Heading for the 21st Century

96 - 215

D

Heading for the 21st Century

951.059
C 365 h

96-215

Publisher: Jason C. Hu
Published by the Government Information Office
2 Tientsin Street, Taipei, Taiwan, ROC

Printed by China Art Printing Works Yu Tai Industrial Corp., Ltd.
6 Pao Ching Road, Hsintien, Taipei County, Taiwan, ROC

Design and Layout: Yen Su-hua
Photographers: Lee Pei-huei   Lu Sha-chou

1st edition, D5   October 1994
Catalog Card No. GIO-EN-BO-83-273-I
ISBN 957-00-4444-6

Printed in the Republic of China on Taiwan
Price: NT$225   US$8.50

Contents

Creating a harmonious society in Taiwan and upgrading the ROC's foreign relations are two of the most important objectives of Premier Lien's administration.

After receiving the premier's seal from his predecessor on February 27, 1993, Dr. Lien began shouldering greater official responsibilities for the nation's administration.

In his first press conference held on the day of his
inauguration, the new ROC
premier outlines his administrative ideals.

$\mathbf{A}$t the 14th national congress
of the Kuomintang held on August 16, 1993, the premier (far
right) poses for a picture with
the ROC President Lee Teng-hui
(center), Vice President Li Yuan-
tsu (second from the left), former
Premier Hau Pei-tsun (second
from the right), and former
President of the Judicial Yuan
Lin Yang-kang (left).

Premier Lien's mother taught
him traditional Chinese values, which he later combined
with the knowledge he ac-
quired from the West to create his own world perspective.

$\mathbf{A}$ happy and harmonious family has been a source of support for the premier throughout his academic and political careers.

Premier Lien enjoys a private moment with family members at his birthday party on August 25, 1993.

Lien Chan

Premier of the Republic of China

Dr. Lien Chan was born in Sian, Shensi Province, on August 27, 1936, during wartime. The only son of a military officer and a teacher, Dr. Lien was sent to a boarding school as a child. In 1946, a year after the return of Taiwan to Chinese rule following 50 years of Japanese occupation, Lien Chan's father, Lien Chen-tung, moved his family back to his hometown in the southern Taiwan city of Tainan. There Lien Chan completed elementary school and went on to junior and senior high schools in Taipei, performing outstandingly well in both studies and sports. Lively and dynamic, he was elected class leader and head of a number of student organizations on several occasions.

In 1953, Lien Chan passed highly competitive university entrance examinations and chose to enroll in the Department of Political Science at National Taiwan University. This first contact with political science led to a lifetime career in politics. In 1959, Lien Chan went to the United States to pursue advanced studies at the University of Chicago, where he earned a master's degree in international law and diplomacy *summa cum laude*. In 1965, he obtained his doctorate in political science also from the University of Chicago. In the same year, he married Fang Yui.

Three years later, Dr. Lien responded to the ROC government's call on overseas scholars to return to Taiwan for public service. He became a visiting professor at the Department of Political Science at his alma mater and was named chairman of the department and the Graduate Institute of Political Science the following year. In 1975, he was appointed ambassador to the Republic of El Salvador. On his first diplomatic mission overseas, Dr. Lien strengthened the ROC's friendly relations with his host country, paving the way for El Salvador's stationing of a permanent ambassador to the ROC.

As recognition of his accomplishments for a man so young, Dr. Lien was reassigned as director of the Department of Youth Affairs of the ruling Kuomintang's Central Committee in 1976. He was promoted to deputy secretary-general of the KMT's Central Committee in 1978. A few months later, he was again called upon to provide expertise and guidance to ROC young people as chairman of the National Youth Commission of the Executive Yuan. He remained in this post until 1981, when he was appointed minister of transportation and communications.

During the next six years, Dr. Lien launched a series of innovative projects that consolidated the groundwork for Taiwan's development into a transportation center for the Asia-Pacific. Global shipping lanes and new air routes were established, domestic and international telecommunication services were upgraded, and the construction of an underground rail network and a modern train station was commenced in Taipei. During this period of diplomatic setbacks following the severance of ROC-U.S. official relations in 1978, Lien Chan encouraged people-to-people diplomacy by lifting overseas travel restrictions for ROC nationals and developing sightseeing spots to attract foreign tourists to Taiwan.

During his tenure as vice premier between 1987 and 1988, Dr. Lien presided over the Environmental Protection Commission, commanded the Hong Kong and Macau Affairs Task Force, and chaired the ad hoc committee on revising the *Organic Law of the Executive Yuan*. The comprehensive understanding of national affairs he developed within this one year was helpful to his later career.

As minister of foreign affairs between 1988 and 1990, Lien Chan set about expanding the ROC's room for international maneuver in keeping with President Lee Teng-hui's policy of pursuing pragmatic diplomacy. Official ties were strengthened and substantive relations were established through economic, trade, and other forms of cooperation. Dr. Lien helped establish the International Economic Cooperation and Development Fund and resumed the ROC's participation in the board activities of the Asian Development Bank. He also set in motion the ROC's entry into the General Agreement on Tariffs and Trade.

Dr. Lien was named governor of Taiwan in June 1990 and committed himself to maintaining balanced development in rural and urban areas. By the end of his nearly three years in office, the living standards in rural areas had been raised, entrepreneurial farm management introduced, and cultural facilities improved. Governor Lien met frequently with local representatives out of concern for communities at the grassroots level, and this enabled him to pinpoint and solve major issues for the people. He also dedicated immense effort to creating a harmonious and peaceful society. His remarkable record of accomplishments earned him a reputation for capable and efficient governance, paving the way for his promotion to the premiership.

When Lien Chan assumed the premiership in 1993, he carried over to the national level of government his ideal of a harmonious society and a multifaceted approach to problem-solving. He quickly demonstrated his ability to handle challenges posed by a reinvigorated democracy, complex relations with the Chinese mainland, a swiftly changing international environment, and intensifying domestic demand for improved living conditions. Backed by his extensive experience and global perspective, he set about establishing in a down-to-earth manner a diverse yet harmonious national community. In just eighteen months, Premier Lien has tackled everything from economics to the environment, from health to education, from social welfare to law and order.

He had been in office a mere three months when he declared an all-out war on drugs. Unlike previous efforts to eradicate drugs, the Lien administration not only clamped down on drug abuse and trafficking but also initiated related educational programs for all. A few weeks later, Premier Lien introduced an Economic Stimulus Package which has revitalized the ROC economy, stimulated private investment, and laid the groundwork for Taiwan's development into a multi-functional regional operations center. At a time when countries around the world are shifting from bipolar confrontation to regional economic alignment, the Lien administration has moved swiftly to expand the ROC's role in the international arena.

The flexibility that President Lee's pragmatic diplomacy allows has been the decisive factor behind the increased number of international activities in which the ROC has participated. As part of an effort to do its share for the global community, the ROC is playing an active role in such regional organizations as the Asia-Pacific Economic Cooperation forum. The Lien administration has become more aggressive in its moves to join GATT and more vocal in its call for a place in the United Nations. Premier Lien has also staunchly maintained a one-China policy while cautiously increasing economic and cultural exchanges with the mainland. Expanded contacts with the civil sector on the other side of the Taiwan Straits have already given rise to a number of problems, leading the premier, in an attempt to protect the interests of Taiwan residents, to initiate a series of bilateral talks with Peking through an intermediary body. Given the mainland regime's unrelenting moves to isolate Taiwan, Premier Lien has repeatedly called on Peking to view cross-Straits relations from a "win-win" perspective rather than as a zero-sum game.

The premier has also taken a number of measures that have lent impetus to Taiwan's advance towards the ranks of developed nations. A redistribution of administrative power to local governments has been assured by legislation, and the governor of Taiwan will be popularly elected beginning this year. The long-awaited national health insurance program will be implemented in January 1995 while concrete plans for a national annuity fund have been drawn up. The educational system is being revamped, athletics is gaining in importance, and more is being spent on environmental protection, wildlife conservation, and scientific research. The series of administrative reforms that Premier Lien has undertaken to slash spending, reduce government personnel levels, and fight corruption have had some success. In June 1994, the United States' Business Environment Risk Intelligence S.A. ranked the ROC government third worldwide in terms of efficiency, next only to Singapore and Switzerland. His unassuming demeanor notwithstanding, the premier has turned out to be a dynamic innovator with a compelling vision of the ROC's future.

Jason C. Hu
Director-General
Government Information Office

I. General Policies

On their way to Central America for a state visit on January 24, 1994, Premier and Mrs. Lien stop over in the United States and are warmly received by former U.S. President Ronald Reagan and his wife.

Where Our Administrative Efforts Must Go

Administrative Report to the First Session of
the Second Legislature
March 12, 1993

In the international community, polarized antagonism has transformed into pluralistic co-existence. Major nations in this world are trying their best to protect
their national interests through regional integration, to
maintain international peace through coordination and
cooperation, and to raise national status through economic strength. The pace of economic growth in the
Asia-Pacific region ranks first in the world, making the
region, along with the European Community and the
North-American Free Trade Zone, the center of gravity
and focus of the world situation. The ever-deepening
economic reform on the Chinese mainland is having a
greater and greater impact on its communist dictatorship, while the increasingly apparent expansion of its
military build-up to achieve regional hegemony has
drawn worldwide attention.

The painstaking efforts of the Republic of China on
Taiwan over the past four decades have fostered democracy and prosperity. Simultaneous political, economic,
and social transformations like those that have occurred
in our nation over the last couple of years, and their
reverberative power, have rarely been seen. As we face
this sort of completely new age full of challenges and

5

hopes, the entire populace is concerned with such questions as: How should we proceed, and how should we continue to develop our economy and forcefully implement democracy while carving out a pivotal position for ourselves in the new international order? How can we work together with one mind to raise the sails and steer the rudder of the grand vessel on which rides the hopes of all Chinese, as it heads against the wind, and braves the waves?

We believe unity is the lifeline of national existence, and the Republic of China's constitutional system is the core of unity. With limited land area and natural resources, we have created a "Taiwan Experience" of rich connotations — a great work which the whole populace — regardless of ethnic background, provincial origin, party affiliation, religious belief, or region, has drafted with wisdom and painted with a brush moistened with blood and sweat. Today our nation's situation is still unfavorable, so we must make it clear that we are all in the same boat. If we succeed, the glory will be shared by each of us. If we fail, all of us must bear the responsibility of failure — no one can escape it. All acts of self-deprecation, division, and isolation are absolutely unwise, for they will bring obvious and immediate dangers upon the nation.

Conceptual and policy controversies among political parties are normal in a democracy. It is also natural for citizens in a pluralistic society to be bold with their opinions about public policies. However, all advocacies and acts should be confined within the framework of the constitutional system, in order not to disperse or sap our national strength, or to fall behind in both overall global competition and that between the two sides of the Taiwan Straits. We should harbor no prejudices or misgivings, especially at this juncture when the task of constitutional reform has just been completed, the status of the nation has thus been determined, the way for party politics paved, and the direction of the policies concerning the people's livelihood has been set in accordance with the will of the entire citizenry.

Furthermore, everyone is full of remorse for unfortunate incidents of history, but only proper ways should be taken to salve the wounds and heal the pain. The significance is to clarify the truth and learn a lesson from it. Only those who can shoulder the responsibility of drawing the people closer through love and tolerance can be considered wise and brave.

We all know that innovation and concrete solutions are the impetus for progress. Over the past forty-odd years, we have developed in accordance with the spirit and essence of the statement in the ROC Constitution, "the Republic of China, founded on the Three Principles of the People, shall be a democratic republic of the people, to be governed by the people and for the people," a set of systems and a spirit suitable for the current situation. The result is a powerful nation and a prosperous society.

The outstanding achievements of our worthy forebears and senior citizens merit our respect and admiration. However, as we carry on with their unfinished tasks, we should broaden our horizons, open our minds, and manifest the creative strength of a modern citizenry. We should totally embrace the venerable, yet eternally new concepts and systems that have stood the test of time, and bring them to new glory. We must also have the courage and determination to renovate old regulations and practices which have become irrelevant to the current situation because of changes in time and perspective. Unless we try, how can we succeed? Confronted with a new situation at home and abroad, we have to face reality squarely and seek breakthroughs cautiously, under the premise of general stability.

We have found that popular will is the basis of administration. Democratic politics is the politics of popular will. Each of you entered this legislative hall with the support of the electorate two months ago — an expression of the latest and most extensive will of the public which we of the administrative branch must of course accord the highest respect. According to statistics, the ten major public policies that most concerned the public during the election of the second-term legislators were: (1) enhancing social welfare, (2) improving educational quality, (3) constructing more public housing to lower housing prices, (4) reforming the tax system, (5) carrying out environmental protection, (6) implementing universal health insurance, (7) properly planning mainland policies, (8) eliminating every kind of special privilege, (9) reinforcing the scale and supervision of the Six-Year National Development Plan, and (10) comprehensively reviewing land policy. The Executive Yuan will make a thorough and careful study of these issues and devise plans to put them into effect.

We maintain that "keeping the big picture in mind" is basic to decision making. Nation and society are one body — internal affairs, national defense, diplomacy, finance and economics, as well as culture and education are its inseparable flesh and blood. By the same token, the relationship between central and local government is just like that between the roots and stalk of a plant, and its leaves and branches. Neither should be dispensed with, but rather, both should simultaneously undergo balanced development.

We believe that conducting administrative affairs in accordance with the law is an iron principle that must be followed. The powers legally invested in administrative institutions shall be properly exercised such that the national rights can be consolidated and the people's rights protected. Those issues that infringe on the rights and obligations of the people must be identified and assessed by the administrative institutions according to the law. Personal prejudices and elements of interest should not be involved. Misuse of power or neglect of responsibility, like violations of the law and dereliction of duty, will not be tolerated. In order to usher in this new development of multi-party politics, administrative neutrality, and a clear-cut distinction between party and government must be the attitude and stance of administrative institutions.

We agree that we must strive for consistency in government policies. My predecessor, Premier Hau Pei-tsun, has, in his loyalty and dedication to the nation, proposed many reform measures, and with great foresight, introduced the Six-Year National Development Plan, all of which are now being implemented. These projects and measures have been formulated after a comprehensive decision-making process and, of course, should be thoroughly implemented as they are closely related to public welfare. In addition, the administrative guidelines for fiscal 1994 have been formulated and will be implemented individually. The fiscal 1994 central government budget has also been drawn up and will soon be submitted to this esteemed legislative body for review. Each of these policies and plans will be implemented unless a change in the situation calls for supplemental addition or revision.

On the basis of these observations, I want to explicitly point out that the ultimate goal of the administration of the Executive Yuan is to develop the Republic of China into a modern and advanced country before the arrival of the 21st century. The concrete targets are:

■ Success in constitutional reform — The legal framework shall have been completed for multi-party politics, as well as a politics based on responsibility, popular will, and the rule of law — which shall function smoothly and maturely.

■ Continued economic prosperity — The gross national product shall have reached US$440 billion, two-way trade shall have climbed to a high of US$300 billion, and per capita income shall exceed US$20,000. The Republic of China on Taiwan shall have become a transportation and transshipment center, a financial hub, and an important zone for science and technology in the Western Pacific region. Anyway you look at it, we shall measure up to the standards of developed countries and shall emerge as an important member of the international economic and trade community.

■ A society of harmony and peace — The entire populace shall be united under the system of constitutional rule. Parochial prejudices and the obsession with provincial origins will be completely dispelled. Social law and order will be maintained. There will be equitable distribution of wealth, and the public will enjoy freedom from fear or want.

■ A robust culture and education — The living environment shall be clean and beautiful. There shall be a widespread and profound interest in culture, arts, and technology. People shall enjoy the living standard of an advanced nation.

■ A powerful and prosperous nation — The country will have a high degree of self-defense capability and tremendous potential for assuming major international responsibilities, in addition to receiving worldwide acceptance and respect.

This is not an unreachable dream, but rather one that can come true. As long as we are prepared to make sacrifices, to pour forth our wisdom and energy, to vigorously follow through on our statements, then these dreams will fully become reality. I have high hopes for all our compatriots and have steadfast confidence in myself and our administrative institutions at all levels.

I will now set forth a summary of the present situation and my future scenario for government administration, sincerely seeking your advice. Since I have just assumed office, I shall hasten to delve into these matters in greater detail later on with each of the ministries in hopes of achieving completeness and comprehensiveness.

Dissemination of Political Democracy

Political democracy is the most important link in national development. Only with political democratization can overall development remain on track without being obscured by the politicization of issues. Therefore, the government has adopted, or will adopt the following measures:

■ To temporize with the nation's political development, laws for self-government in provinces and counties as well as in special municipalities are being drafted in accordance with the provisions of the Constitution and its Additional Articles. We hope to revise and formulate pertinent regulations for local self-government by the end of this June in coordination with the legislation of these bills, thereby implementing local self-government and accelerating political reform.

■ In coordination with the implementation of the *Statute for the Security and Guidance of the Kinmen, Matsu, Tungsha and Nansha Areas,* military rule of Kinmen was terminated on November 7, 1992, and local self-government is gradually being implemented.

■ Members of the Second Legislative Yuan have been elected, and there have been clear improvements in the unsavory intrusion of violence and money into elections. This is sufficient testimony to the maturity of democratic concepts among the electorate and the candidates. Of course, there is more to be desired. We shall take counsel from various circles in order to make necessary revisions to the *Public Officials' Election and Recall Law.*

■ The maintenance of law and order will be stepped up. According to statistics, violent crimes have decreased in recent years and the overall crime situation has shown signs of improvement. But the criminal population continues to grow as the average criminal age falls. This is a warning sign that cannot be ignored. It is the responsibility of the prosecuting and police institutions to dedicate their efforts to putting an end to this phenomenon. We must also fundamentally eliminate the factors behind the commission of crime through various means such as education, code of ethics, and family relations. Follow-up police administration plans should be reviewed at appropriate times to ensure the anticipated results.

■ All such laws, administrative orders, and regulations that do not conform to democracy, the rule of law and human rights shall be revised posthaste lest they become obstacles to progress. The law on political parties will be speedily initiated after a consensus has been achieved. Rulings on administrative relief of petitions and complaints shall be made in accordance with the law and from the vantage of the people's suffering, but equal care shall be taken that government authority is properly exercised and private rights are well protected.

■ In order to set a legal framework for the zoning of administrative districts, research will be conducted and an administrative district zoning bill drafted in accordance with the Constitution. I hope that the legislative proceedings on this bill can be completed before the end of this June. Then we can actively go about rezoning administrative districts, promoting balanced regional development, reducing the differences between urban and rural areas, and creating an ideal living environment for the people.

■ Research will be prudently conducted on our land policy to solve land problems. Basically, the equalization of land rights envisioned by Dr. Sun Yat-sen should still serve as the highest guiding principle in the solution of land-related issues. This will be directed at stabilizing land prices and remitting the increase in land values to the public.

Promoting Pragmatic Foreign Relations

Faced with an increasingly complex and variegated global environment where practical interests reign supreme, as well as with pressure on us from the Chinese communists, I would like to stress that we will adhere to the "one China" principle stipulated in the *Guidelines for National Unification*, and to the stance that the ROC is a sovereign state, and accept the objective and present reality of a temporary division between the two sides of the Taiwan Straits. With a pragmatic attitude, we will also make good use of our trading and economic might to compete for the friendship of other nations, strengthen cooperative relations with countries that already have diplomatic ties with the ROC, enhance the substantive relations with countries that lack diplomatic links with us, and widen our participation in international organizations and activities so as to dispel the outdated concept of a growth and decline of the relative strength of the two sides of the Taiwan Straits.

In this regard, we have had some great achievements in the past. For example, relations between the ROC and friendly countries in Central and South America remain very sincere; relations with the United States, Japan, and Europe are proceeding on a normal track; and the development of relations between the ROC and Russia, Israel, Vietnam, and east European countries have taken the first step forward. At present, the ROC has established official diplomatic ties with 29 countries around the world and has set up representative offices in

59 countries that lack diplomatic relations with the ROC. Among these representative offices, 17 even bear the name "Republic of China."

In addition, we have scored breakthroughs in purchasing weapons from foreign countries as well as establishing mutual aviation rights. Moreover, our application to GATT has been accepted for review, and many ranking officials from the United States, Germany, France, and other countries have visited Taiwan over the past few years. All these are signs of a positive response from the international community to ROC pragmatic diplomacy. Therefore, the ROC should set a return to international society as the ultimate goal of its diplomatic affairs.

Strengthening National Defense Capability

Based on the understanding that national security is more important than anything else, so, we shall adhere to our directive of waging war in self-defense, and shall implement an elite troop concept, make adjustments in our military strength and configuration, improve the quality of personnel, and develop and purchase additional high-tech weapons and equipment in order to upgrade both our tangible and intangible fighting capabilities. We shall also establish a coastal patrol headquarters and transfer some troops from the army and military police, and reorganize them into a coastal garrison (police) force to carry out the mission of coastal defense. In addition, the ratio between the number of officers, noncommissioned officers, and enlisted personnel will be adjusted to 1:3:2 so as to streamline military personnel. We shall also promote cooperation among the armed forces, public organizations, and the private sector to jointly participate in national defense industry research, development, and production.

We shall also initiate a legal framework for the national defense structure and enhance military education. President Lee once stated that, "when it comes to national security, no mere material construction can substitute for the awesome spiritual power drawn from a base of national consciousness. At present, the speeches and misleading advocacies of a minority of people calling for splitting the territory of our nation not only might create internal divisiveness and affect social harmony and security, but might even lead to a reversal in relations between the two sides of the Taiwan Straits. They really only bring myriad harm, without producing a single benefit. I hope that all of the citizenry will be profoundly and keenly aware of what is right, will carefully weigh the costs and benefits, stand together through thick and thin, and reach the consensus that we all share a common destiny with each other. Only by doing so can our national security be most powerfully guaranteed." We should deeply ponder the meaning of President Lee's words and then do our best to start working on our tasks.

Speedily Developing the Economy

Over the past year, the ROC achieved an economic growth rate of approximately 6.1 percent, per capita GNP of US$10,200, and total trade of more than US$153 billion. With the entire world in an economic slump, for Taiwan to establish such an excellent performance was especially praiseworthy. Looking to this year, the Six-Year National Development Plan is comprehensively underway, domestic demand continues to expand, and the world economic situation can be expected to recover. The 1993 economic growth target has been set at seven percent, with per capita GNP to possibly rise to as high as US$11,000. The distance remaining before the ROC joins the ranks of developed nations will have been further closed.

In order to realize these preset goals, we will strive to follow the main points listed below:

■ Fully implement the policy of economic liberalization. We shall reduce tariffs, relax limitations on outward investment and on foreigners investing in Taiwan, plan the establishment of Taiwan as an international financial center and a transportation hub for the Western Pacific, and enthusiastically participate in international trade organizations and activities.

■ Improve the investment climate. We shall actively re-adjust industrial areas; continue to develop the offshore island basic industrial areas, sci-tech industrial areas and software industrial areas in Changpin and Yünlin; study and draft preferential tariff and financial measures; and give dedicated assistance to companies to solve their difficulties; and encourage private-sector willingness to invest.

■ Upgrade industry. We shall open up key technologies and develop newly-arising industries, promote industrial automation, encourage research and development, spur the modernization of commerce and traditional industries, assist small and medium-sized businesses in improving their infrastructures, liberalize the financial markets, and enhance transportation facilities.

■ Realize the principle of fair trade. We shall balance our trade development, cautiously deal with talks concerning our admittance to GATT, adjust our trade policies, pay equal heed to the demands of industrial development, protect intellectual property rights, and most of all, work to diversify our foreign trade markets.

While our trade surplus with the U.S. is being gradually reduced annually, our trade deficit with Japan continues to widen and this must be improved. The government agencies in charge will be asked to take concrete actions to raise our product quality and design capability. And in coordination, we will step up promotional activities to open up the Japanese market for our products. At the same time, we shall provide guidance to local manufacturers on setting up major component industries and to diversify import sources in order to reduce the independence on Japan and achieve structural change.

■ Go all out to stabilize commodity prices. Although last year's import and export prices and wholesale prices were all relatively lower than those of the previous year, consumer prices rose by 4.5 percent. This was because the prices of foodstuffs were affected by natural disasters. If foodstuff prices were not included, the increase was only 2.8 percent, which is still in a tolerable range. This year, we are striving for the goal of keeping price increases under 3.5 percent. Accordingly, the government will meticulously handle the timing and extent of price adjustments for public services and enterprises, and by following the path of regulating finances and ensuring a sufficient supply of goods and materials, will dispel the psychology of anticipating price rises.

■ Make agricultural development sound. With integral, local and global considerations in mind, we shall hasten modifications to the production and marketing structure of agriculture, raise agricultural production efficiency, increase the income of farmers, and improve the living environment in farming villages so as to achieve the policy goals of developing agriculture, building up farming villages, and taking care of farmers. All sectors have reached a consensus on setting up a farmer's annuity system. Its manner of implementation and coverage is actively being planned and deliberated. Furthermore, we are making preparations in advance for any possible impact on agriculture from ROC admission into GATT in order to protect the livelihood and interests of the farming populace.

■ Harmonize relations between labor and management, advance ethical relations between labor and management, and guarantee the rights and interests of laborers so that labor and management will be as one, reaping the same gains and sharing the same losses.

Expanding Our Mainland Policy

The ideals, principles and course of our mainland policy have been clearly stated in the *Guidelines for National Unification*. Implementation of the measures and regulations for our mainland policy has also been fulfilled by the *Statute Governing the Relations Between the People of the Taiwan Area and the People of the Mainland Area*. Administrative agencies should adhere to these guidelines and carry them out in proper sequence without haste.

Toward the end of 1987, the government of the Republic of China permitted people from the Taiwan area to visit relatives on the mainland, marking the inception of new relations between the two sides of the Taiwan Straits. For the past five years, trade, economic and cultural exchanges between people from both sides of the Straits have taken greater strides and have grown in magnitude. There is a greater degree of mutual reciprocity, and a strengthening of mutual trust, fostering a new opportunity for national unification.

Presently, we are stepping up research and planning of an integrated mainland policy, expanding cross-Straits cultural exchanges and mapping out on a step-by-step basis economic and trade activities between the two sides of the Straits. As for Taiwan businesses going to the mainland, we are moving toward liberalization in the long-term phase, while in the near-term phase we are proceeding in the direction of equally stressing guidance and regulation. We hope that these measures will produce mutually beneficial effects, and will help upgrade local industries as well as assist economic reform on the mainland.

Although we are tremendously confident and sincere about national unification, and respect the status of Chinese communist authorities on the mainland, the Chinese communists have always belittled the reality of the existence of the Republic of China on Taiwan. They harp on the "one China, two systems" premise, and thus relations between the two sides of the Straits continue to be stuck in a state of mitigated hostility, unable to further proceed toward the mid-term phase of "mutual cooperation" as outlined in the *Guidelines for National Unification*. Consequently, communication at the official-level, and direct postal, transport and commercial links cannot be realized. We profoundly hope that the Chinese communists can get out of their traditional rut of "struggle between the Nationalists and Communists," and instead strive from a new perspective — that of the long-term benefit of the Chinese race and the trend of the times. Only then can the impasse be broken and a new situation emerge.

President Lee once pointed out, "The rending of the nation is an unfortunate historical event. We can only heal this historical wound through adherence to the spirit of 'the world is for all'; by abandoning all personal and political self-interest, and genuinely having in mind the future of China and the welfare of the Chinese people." Those on both sides of the Straits should solemnly consider the words of wisdom.

Promoting National Construction

The Six-Year National Development Plan has already entered its third year. It is proceeding smoothly, both in terms of planning and execution. Of the 64 projects that require expenditures exceeding US$20 billion, 19 are still being planned, while work has already started on the remaining 45.

The Six-Year National Development Plan is an important avenue to modernization, so we must step up its implementation hereafter. However, we must still give consideration to the financial burden incurred, and to our planning and execution capabilities. Every fiscal year when we allocate and plan the budget, necessary financial adjustments or additional appropriations will be made. In principle, we shall give priority to projects with growth potential, and leave the non-productive ones for further study and deliberation.

The expenditures required for the Six-Year National Development Plan are enormous. We shall follow the policies of eliminating waste, encouraging participation by the private sector, promoting a user-pay system, expediting the privatization of national enterprises and the appropriate use of public bonds. We shall raise the requisite capital through opening up new sources of income and cutting expenses. However, we shall absolutely not enlarge the budget deficit to avoid endangering the soundness of the financial system.

Occupying one-third of the total budget for the Six-Year National Development Plan, infrastructural development of transportation is of utmost importance. We are actively implementing such extension projects as the high-speed railway, the Second Northern Freeway and the second freeway; Taipei-Ilan Freeway; the West Coast Highway projects; and the twelve highways along the western corridor. All such projects are either planned or actively underway. We should set zero defects in their construction and quality control as our goal.

Revitalizing Culture and Education

Education and culture are the deep structure of national development. For years, the government has poured in enormous amounts of manpower and resources — implementing nine-year compulsory education, opening up more colleges and universities, establishing technical and vocational educational systems, bolstering social education, promoting the development of science and technology, and setting up agencies with the special responsibility of working for the rejuvenation of culture — to cultivate a healthy citizenry and talented people for the nation, and as well develop modern Chinese culture. We see a multitude of bold and decisive businessmen of keen vision active in the international arena. We see many scholars and experts in their 30s and 40s contributing their wisdom in academic areas and various lines of businesses. We see that the majority of citizens have their own opinions with regard to public policy and are equipped with sound learning capabilities and democratic skills. We see that small and medium-sized businesses are capable of adjusting their business configurations and strategies at the right time and emerge stronger from formidable challenges and difficulties. These allow us to more clearly apprehend the vitality that flows from the "Taiwan Experience." For the successes in education and culture, we want to express deep satisfaction and appreciation.

Nonetheless, there are quite a few latent problems remaining in education and culture. Important examples include the cause and effect connection between the method of instruction in elementary schools and the increasing crime rate among teenagers and young people, the need to pay equal attention to the quality and quantity of colleges and universities, the status of vocational schools and the employment prospects for their students, and the distinction between vulgar and popular culture. Each of these issues is of great concern all around, and should urgently be addressed.

In the future, we shall require agencies in charge to especially pay attention to respect for academic freedom, upgrading the atmosphere for research, improving

23

our technical and vocational education systems, establishing campus ethics, enhancing the meaningfulness of national education, promoting physical education, making cultural facilities accessible, and harmoniously blending refined culture with popular culture, and traditional culture with modern living. We shall also step up our efforts for science and technology to take root and be integrated with industrial production.

Improving Our Quality of Life

The purpose of economic development is to improve the national quality of life. When I examine our current economic strength, I believe it can provide sustaining power for the following issues:

■ The environment of the Taiwan area is heavily burdened and should not be damaged further. It is urgently necessary to improve the current state of pollution and prevent the production of new pollutants, so as to effectively control and reduce public harm to the environment. Important measures include actively carrying out waste reduction and retrieval, the recycling of resources, constructing waste management plants and incinerators, and strict control of industrial pollution sources. It is anticipated that by the year 2000, the quality of the ROC environment can be raised to standards already in effect now in other highly developed nations. Furthermore, in order to fulfill our international obligations, we shall urge our domestic industrial structure to meet the demands of environmental protection, and speed up the elimination and replacement of chlorofluorocarbons, as well as control of sulfur dioxide emissions.

■ Actively map out a universal national insurance program which it is hoped can be implemented next year, equalize and enhance medical facilities, step up the prevention and control of drug abuse, safeguard the sanitary condition of foods and beverages, reinforce the system of disease control, and research and draft the Six-year National Health Care Plan to reduce the incidence of chronic and degenerative diseases, and improve the health of citizens in every age bracket.

■ Establish and build national parks, as well as advocate appropriate recreational activities.

■ Beautify the urban landscape, safeguard public safety, promote community development, rectify manners and customs, and advocate athletic activities to develop the character of citizens, strengthen their bodies, and promote social peace and harmony.

Enhancing Social Welfare

We have adopted a progressive social welfare system for implementation. As for social insurance, universal national health insurance is slated to be completed by 1994, and an annuity program is also under preliminary review along with the insurance system. Prior to the implementation of these, the farmers', labor, and government employees' insurance programs should be improved in accordance with the spirit of balancing income and expenditures, and sharing risk, and should differ somewhat from social welfare in the narrow sense.

We shall increase living cost subsidies for low-income people so they can maintain a subsistence level of living, offering employment in exchange for welfare

25

payments, and granting school allowances to their children, so as to encourage them to fend for themselves, and ultimately shed poverty. We should take good care of elderly people without means of support, the severely handicapped, chronically ill patients, and the totally incapacitated. We should step up protection for women, children, and young people, and assist the development of their minds and bodies.

Moreover, we shall expand construction of national housing units to help solve the living problems of low- and middle-income citizens. Construction of 9,000 units is planned for this year, of which 4,500 units will be directly built by the government. In addition, we shall ensure the rights and benefits of veterans and aborigines, and provide them with the appropriate assistance and guidance.

It is an indisputable fact that our level of social welfare is not in line with the level of our national income. From now on, governments at all levels should increase their social welfare budgets to the maximum of their financial capabilities, and increase their services. However, once social welfare programs are underway, this will be a long-term burden for the government — that is to say — the whole citizenry. Therefore, we must be prudent at the outset and plan our financing sources and program details well, to avoid wastefulness or distorting the distribution of social resources, which would hinder the pace of national development.

In addition, there has been a trend toward a widening in the social gap between rich and poor in recent years — to which we should really pay close attention.

In addition to redistributing wealth by the way of tax collection, a sound social welfare system can also eliminate poverty. When the vast majority of people become moderately well-off, the severity of the gap between poor and wealthy will accordingly be diminished.

Making the Financial and Banking System Sound

The soundness of the financial and banking system is an indispensable prerequisite for national development. The important tasks for the government are:

■ To spur the rationalization of central and local government finances, and gradually increase the number of autonomous finance sources for local governments.

■ To make the tax system sound and improve tax administration in line with the social justice of levying taxes according to ability and fairness of tax burden.

■ To regulate the finance system, maintain an appropriate money supply, and promote price stability.

■ Make the stock market and foreign exchange markets sound, as well as strengthen management of government bonds and state-owned land.

Raising Administrative Efficiency

The pace of a nation's modernization is closely connected with the administrative efficiency of its government. In light of my duty and my personal conscience, I am determined to do my utmost to establish an honest, fair, and moreover, efficient government.

First of all, the legislative process for the "Sunshine Bill" should be completed as quickly as possible, so that activities by politicians and political groups will take place in the open to dispel public apprehensions about the involvement of wealth and privilege in politics, and about the conveyance of benefits. Those who participate in politics, on the other hand, should be accorded the faith and dignity they deserve.

Secondly, the organization of administrative agencies and number of their employees should be studied in depth, to prevent unreasonable expansion or increases. Organizational expansion or an increase in the number of employees of any newly established agency shall be subject to prudent consideration. The *Executive Yuan Organic Law* shall be amended to keep abreast with the times, and match the needs of society. The amendment shall, after careful study, be made in line with the principles of organization and division of labor. We should encourage and assist the private sector to handle matters that are within its capabilities, or that are suitable for it to deal with. It is manifestly unreasonable for the average person to use whether or not the government has established an agency with designated responsibilities underneath the Executive Yuan as a criterion for weighing the extent to which the government regards a particular issue as important.

The functions of agencies of a secretarial or advisory nature, such as the Directorate-General of Budget, Accounting and Statistics; the Central Personnel Administration; the Research, Development and Evaluation Commission; and the Government Information Office should be strengthened to render assistance in formulating, promoting, examining and reviewing policies.

Distinguished legislators, we are now standing at a crossroads concerning the future of our nation and race: If we grasp current trends and create favorable opportunities for ourselves, unite, and strive together, we shall lead our country to a prosperous, healthy and happy modernity. But if we only give lip service to these ideas and bicker among ourselves, merely drifting with the tide, then our nation shall sink into poverty and isolation, even to the point of endangering its very existence. The fate of our country lies in our own hands. Which way we shall go and what kind of lifestyle we want to choose are decisions to be made by the 20 million people living in the free area of China and by their government organized according to the Five-power Constitution of the Republic of China. The duties and responsibilities of our administrative departments are most complex and heavy, and especially require the exertion of even greater painstaking effort and wisdom. What I ask and require of myself is to:

First, abide by my conscience — All that I do must not only conform to laws and regulations, but must even more accord with moral standards. I demand of myself that my actions at all times are those for which I never need feel shame, and that my heart is clear and at ease.

Second, display sincerity — When facing divergent voices and appeals, I must not only have the courage to insist on my position concerning cardinal issues of right and wrong but also the humble forbearance to listen to others with mutual respect. The national interest and the welfare of the people must come before my personal interest or partisan considerations of gain or losses. I must eliminate conflict and transform differences into agreement by my display of utmost sincerity.

Third, extend forth love — Love is the most wonderful and precious of all feelings. Starting with the love felt for family, parents, and children, it should be extended forth to friends, community members, and compatriots, so as to build a society full of love and caring.

The bugle heralding departure has sounded, the gun signaling the start of the race has been fired. Let us bravely strive for pre-eminence, and march toward the goal of becoming a modernized nation before the arrival of the 21st century.

Premier Lien welcomes Mr. and Mrs. Mikhail Gorbachev during their visit to the Republic of China on March 21, 1994.

An Administrative Outline for the New Age

Administrative Report to the Second Session of
the Second Legislature
September 24, 1993

The government administration has always been aimed at developing Taiwan and rebuilding China, and bringing about unification under a system of democracy, freedom and equal distribution of wealth through modernization already realized here on our Bastion of National Revival. After serving as premier for a half year, observing the world situation, and studying public opinion, I deeply feel that realizing the goal of consistent administration requires ensuring the following concrete standards:

■ National progress: We must bring about a democratic political order, maintain a prosperous economy, highly develop our culture, and gain the respect and attention of the international community.

■ Popular content: Materially, all compatriots are content with their basic living necessities and mentally, are peaceful and comfortable, with hopes for the future.

■ Healthy society: In the diversity of a pluralistic society, there is a code of behavior acceptable to all. Thus, we shall reach a consensus of building an organismic community based on respect for individual free will. Furthermore, while our environment is changing rapidly, we have the ability for profound insight and self-reflection, and are full of creative vitality.

33

I realize that in a democratic country and pluralistic society, government administration must be adapted to the environment and follow the public opinion to ensure efficiency. Therefore, in carrying out our administrative tasks, we must adhere to the following principles:

First, standing firm on principles. The Constitution states that "The Republic of China, founded on the Three Principles of the People, shall be a democratic republic of the people, to be governed by the people, and for the people." All of our legal systems and measures should conform with this grand principle, with no deviations or omissions. A country of ideals and principles is a country of hope and dignity. A country that has lost its ideals and principles has lost its justification for existence and its impetus for development. Therefore, no matter how the situation develops, our stance on consolidating the constitutional system and carrying out the Three Principles of the People will never change.

Second, being pragmatic and going back to basics. At present, our society is more concerned with style than substance, rights than obligations, theories than realization, subjective wishes than objective rules. People are loath to sow the seeds but are eager to reap the harvest. Everyone wants to consume, but few like to produce. This has led to a sense of uncertainty throughout the society, posing a great hindrance to modernization. We must correct this perverse tendency right on its root by cultivating the ethos of going back to basics. "Being pragmatic" means facing the fact, speaking sincerely, and doing things honestly. The idea is not to just be fussy about appearances but to really see results. To attain a high quality of life, we must first create high efficiency and productivity. "Going back to basics" means basing the policies on public opinion, promoting national unification on the foundation of Taiwan, Penghu, Kinmen and Matsu, and carrying out national development by first stimulating the willingness to invest and produce.

Third, ensuring unity and harmony. Today, our 21 million compatriots living on Taiwan, Penghu, Kinmen and Matsu share their fate and prosperity, honor and humility. They may differ in views, but their patriotism, love for their homeland, and fondness for their present way of life are the same. Our resources and territory are very limited. The only way for us to survive and develop is to pull ourselves together. As our party politics gains maturity, all disputes can be settled through democratic and systematic procedures. Any divisive or polarizing advocacy is unscrupulous to the extreme, unreasonable, and ultimately harmful to the interests of the people as a whole.

Fourth, seeking innovation and progress. Government changes as the times change, and must continuously reform, adjust its steps to closely conform to public opinion and trends, and produce extraordinary political and economic achievements. Constitutional reform in recent years has accomplished a peaceful revolution that has been affirmed both at home and abroad. But right now, the government has heavy responsibilities and a long way to go. The scale and extent of reform should be enlarged to keep pace with the world and public opinion so that we can gain an advantageous position in cross-Straits and global economic competition.

Over the past half year, the executive branch has carried out its administrative tasks according to the above-mentioned goals and ideals. Its concrete measures and results have been detailed in a written report which has already been forwarded to this distinguished body for perusal by each legislator. In order to make it more understandable, I would like to further explain certain important points and to invite your advice.

Expanding Democratic and Constitutional Politics

Democracy is our most important recourse to seize a foothold in the world democratic camp and win the minds at home and abroad. Over the past three years, we have overcome obstacle after obstacle, and, with reasonable methods and a responsible attitude, have both promoted constitutional reform and established a framework for democracy that should totally succeed in the next few years. From now on, our major task is to embed the constitutional articles in laws and the legal system, to incorporate them in our political activities, and to plant them in the thought and life of our people. The executive branch has drafted the *Self-governance Law for Provinces and Counties*, the *Self-governance Law for Special Municipalities* and the *Redistricting Law for Administrative Areas* and has submitted them to this distinguished body for examination, in hopes that the legislative procedures can be completed before the end of this year. This should enable planning of elections for the governor of Taiwan Province and the mayors of Taipei and Kaohsiung and the study and drafting of pertinent regulations concerning the administration and oversight of self-governance. In addition, we are carefully examining and revising the *Public Officials Election and Recall Law* so that all political parties can compete fairly, justly and openly on a legal basis. At the same time, we are about to study the laws governing lobbying and monetary political contributions, in line with the implementation of the *Public Functionary Assets Disclosure Law*, to put a stop to the involvement of money and violence in elections and to ensure the quality of democratic politics. The election of mayors and county chiefs at the end of this year will be clean and peaceful, setting a new milestone for electoral practices in our nation.

Establishing an Honest and Efficient Government

Ever since the ROC government moved its seat to Taiwan, it constantly has devoted itself to eliminating corruption, raising efficiency, and carrying out administrative reform, thereby facilitating national progress and prosperity. Nevertheless, in view of the rapid changes in political and social development both domestically and internationally, the general public of our nation harbors high expectations for the quality and quantity of governmental administration. To fulfill these expectations and to adapt to the requirements of the environment, the executive branch has introduced an administrative reform bill for implementation. The purpose of this plan is to establish a clean and efficient government. The plan is built on the cornerstones of honesty, efficiency and public convenience.

To achieve honest government, we have moved simultaneously to eliminate corruption, prevent corruption, and revise laws to ensure that government employees at all levels dare not, can not, do not, and need not be corrupt. Concrete measures include:

■ Raising the maximum reward to NT$6 million for an informer. This not only encourages our people to report illicit activities but also indicates the determination of the government to impose stiff penalties for corruption.

■ Zeroing in on 14 categories which are easily involved in corrupt practices, including major construction projects, big-ticket procurements, taxation, police, judiciary/justice affairs, and construction administration. Related government employees are subject to rigorous investigation and prosecution for passing on benefits, demanding kickback payments, accepting payoffs, or other corrupt activities.

■ Increasing penalties for those convicted of corruption, while increasing the number of those who turn themselves in and confess to corruption through the inducement of reduced or suspended sentences.

■ Setting reasonable standards for giving or receiving money or gifts, and the participation in banquets or other social activities by government employees.

■ Establishing a system to deal with the peddling of undue influence.

To raise administrative efficiency, emphasis will be placed on:

■ Tidying up the organization and trimming the payroll of the government to attain the three-year goal of a 5 percent reduction in the total number of employees in the Executive Yuan and its subordinate organizations;

■ Bolstering cultivation and training of manpower at the basic level, promoting overall administrative ability training for management, and fostering medium- and high-level personnel.

■ Establishing a participation-and-suggestion system, correcting work concepts, raising the work morale, and implementing goal-oriented management. Supervisory personnel at all levels are expected to take full responsibility for the reform, and to fashion a new organizational culture.

■ Continuing the promotion of work simplification by dispersing responsibilities, shortening the work flow, simplifying paperwork, and increasing counter services to save the public's time spent on filing applications.

■ Promoting automation and computerization in administrative offices to increase efficiency in processing paperwork, and developing a one-stop counter service system.

■ Accelerating the review and revision of various laws and bolstering the functioning of the rule of law to meet societal demand.

■ Carefully preparing the government budget, stepping up early administrative planning, and drawing up a restraint system for annual government expenditures in order to make proper use of national resources.

The main points of stepping up governmental service to the public include:

■ Requiring all government agencies to select and improve specific services to the public that fall within the scope of their responsibility, and to plan how to carry them out.

■ Requiring all government agencies to strengthen their training and concepts about rendering services based on public wishes, and improve their public service attitudes.

■ Selecting 14 items as principal service concerns, including computerizing household registration, improving hospital service, and allowing more private agencies to inspect privately-owned cars.

To implement the plan, the government will push forward a reform campaign, calling for the "participation of government employees at all levels as one entity." Accordingly, an Administrative Reform Committee will be established in the executive branch, and an Administrative Reform Task Force will be set up in all ministries, provincial and municipal governments. Both are responsible for the promotion and implementation of the reform plan. The goals we have set shall be completed successfully, and no failure will be tolerated. We are going to establish a highly efficient government of good image, which will lead the nation toward advancement and increase the public welfare.

Government employees must display the spirit of sacrifice and dedication and take a firm stand to push administrative measures, fulfill their duties, and complete their missions strictly according to the law. These employees constitute the backbone of our national progress. I am very proud of the numerous high-caliber people working for our government agencies, who, I believe, will also receive appreciation from the public. In addition, I hope that all government employees will further come to understand the situation our nation faces and the aspirations of the public, and, under the premise of adopting new concepts, courageously fulfill their duties. Government employees should never be satisfied with the way things have been done, but rather attain the goal of simplifying administration and offering more convenience to the public. This will brighten the image of the government and enhance their sense of pride and honor. On the other hand, I also hope that all sectors of society will give government employees encouragement and care to raise their morale.

Expanding Our Mainland Policy

Whereas the *Guidelines for National Unification* constitute the framework for our mainland policy, the *Statute Governing Relations Between People of the Taiwan Area and the Mainland Area* set the criteria for the policy. Although we adhere to the one-China principle, we also acknowledge the fact that the Chinese mainland and Taiwan are ruled by two different political entities. Therefore, the two sides of the Taiwan Straits should, based on a stance of parity and mutual respect, reduce hostility by promoting exchanges and fostering cooperation through mutual trust. Once the gap between their political, economic, and social development is reduced, unification can gradually be attained through negotiation by democratic and peaceful means.

With this conviction, our government is devoting itself to the expansion of cultural and academic exchanges, and building complementary economic relations for the benefit of both sides. In addition, intermediary bodies of both sides have held talks and negotiations to deal with problems resulting from private-sector exchanges. However, the groundwork laid by the Koo-Wang Talks, held in Singapore during April 1993 between the chairman of the Straits Exchange Foundation and his counterpart in the Association for Relations Across the Taiwan Straits, led to no progress at a follow-up meeting of the two sides held at the end of August 1993 in Peking.

Instead, Chinese communist authorities published a white paper titled *The Taiwan Question and Reunification of China*, reiterating their "one country, two systems" argument. They have fastidiously sought to denigrate our status in the international community, and have demanded that the ROC government hold "party-to-party negotiations," in an attempt to unreasonably oversimplify the China issue as a "Taiwan question." This regrettable move ignores the historical reality and is tantamount to erecting a new wall right in the midst of gradually improving relations between the two sides of the Taiwan Straits. Nevertheless, we will not deviate from the direction of national unification, nor throw off the pace of exchanges and reciprocity. History will surely prove that the ROC's mainland policy is most capable of not only serving the long-term interests of the Chinese people but also protecting the rights and interests of the 21 million people living in the Taiwan area. I hope all our citizenry will staunchly support, jointly participate in, and actively promote this plan to create favorable conditions for enhancing the welfare of the people on both sides of the Taiwan Straits, and reaching the goal of building a free and democratic China with equitable prosperity.

Strengthening National Defense and Foreign Relations

The survival of a nation is contingent on its military strength, and the growth of a nation necessarily depends on having a wide scope of international activities.

The main mission of the ROC's military policy in the current phase is defense of the Taiwan, Penghu, Kinmen and Matsu area. With the conviction "to rely not on the likelihood of the enemy not coming, but on our own readiness for the fight," the ROC is establishing a military strength capable of guarding the nation and protecting its people. Concrete measures have included:

- implementing an elite troop policy and building the military through austerity and hard work;

- increasing combat readiness with the aim of ensuring the security of the Taiwan Straits by counteracting blockades and expanding the depth of our aerial defense through anti-aircraft interception;

- effectively providing military education, and consolidating military power at the basic levels of the armed forces;

- improving logistic management to meet the demands of combat readiness;

- developing military technology and promoting cooperation with the industrial sector;

- reinforcing group discipline and patriotism among officers and men, and boosting the morale of the army, navy, and air force.

We will make every effort to speed up our progress towards the goal of military modernization. The government guarantees that its strong army, navy, and air force can provide the nation with fortress-like security that safeguards the lives and property of the people in the Taiwan area.

Today the ROC wields great economic and trade strength and occupies a pivotal position in the Asia-

Pacific region. The ROC is the world's 14th largest trading nation, seventh largest investor nation, and one of the foremost holders of foreign exchange reserves. The ROC is in a position to tip the balance on the international scene and serves as a model to neighboring countries in the region with its exceptional achievements in constitutional reform. The Chinese communists have, however, stepped up their boycotts and threats against the ROC, excluding the ROC and attempting to back us into a corner within the international community. The Chinese communists have offended the dignity of the people in the free Taiwan area and disparaged the ROC's international status, thereby undermining prosperity in the Asia-Pacific region and world peace.

The ROC has always clung to its conviction that the two sides of the Taiwan Straits can be unified. The ROC also admits that in the current phase the ROC government cannot effectively exercise jurisdiction over the Chinese mainland. Yet, the ROC is adamant that the simultaneous coexistence of the ROC and the Chinese communist authorities prior to unification be recognized as an indisputable reality. Both sides are entitled to an appropriate international status and to enjoying the same scope of international activities. Based on this conviction, the ROC is consolidating group strength, solidifying the basis of diplomacy, advocating substantive relations, and expanding participation in international organizations in keeping with the principles of equality, reciprocity, independence, autonomy and pragmatism. Over the last half year, impressive results have been made in the areas of international cooperation, talks on aviation rights, and arms purchases.

The ROC strongly desires to draw on its achievements in democratic politics and in economic and trade development as the means to pay back the international community for its help in the past. This desire matches well with the U.N. principle of the universalization of membership and the United Nations' increasing role in recent years of orchestrating and protecting world peace. The ROC participation in the U.N. is a common wish of the people, a right that cannot be cast aside and a responsibility which must not be evaded. The government is committed to building a positive international environment and backing in the United Nations, in the hope of seeing tangible results over the next few years.

By making the mistake of strongly objecting to the ROC's moves to participate in the United Nations, the Chinese communists are actually contradicting the spirit of the U.N. Charter, opposing international reality, and exerting an adverse effect on national integrity. The ROC has repeatedly asserted that it is entitled to an appropriate international status prior to the unification of this nation. The ROC's policy of participating in the United Nations was never meant to create a permanent split between the two sides of the Taiwan Straits. Conversely, the ROC's participation in the United Nations will increase confidence in national unification, and trigger more active measures leading to it. The cases of West and East Germany and North and South Korea are clear precedents. The long-term exclusion of the ROC from the United Nations is surely injurious to the union and development of the Chinese populace. The Chinese communists should not take the hegemonic stand and unreasonably oppose our participation. At the same time, I want to emphasize that as we are in the right, we will not be deferred from this goal.

Because overseas Chinese passionately love their free motherland, the ROC government will serve them with sincerity and in a pragmatic attitude. Further, we will consolidate their strength and make it into a major help in the development of economy and cross-Straits relations and in our bid to participate in the international community.

Promoting National Development

The Six-Year National Development Plan constitutes the blueprint for our nation's modernization. Implementation of the Plan has already produced impressive results. Nonetheless, we have encountered a number of problems. The executive branch is in the process of holding mid-term reviews, considering both the supply side and the demand side in a realistic attitude. The plan has gone through evaluation first by the planning committee, then by the supervisory organizations in the central government and finally by the Council for Economic Planning and Development. It has been thoroughly discussed and examined by relevant organizations. As a result, the 775 projects in the Six-Year National Development Plan have been reduced to 632. The original budget of NT$8,238.2 billion has also been scaled down to NT$6,029.4 billion, roughly NT$3,851.9 billion of which will be required during the 1995 to 1997 fiscal years.

For the next three fiscal years (1995-1997), the public sector of the plan has an available monetary supply of NT$2,847.5 billion against an estimated demand of NT$3,851.9 billion. If, however, the 78 projects which have not yet been approved are taken out of the Six-Year National Development Plan, the budgetary demand would be reduced to NT$3,238.8 billion. The government shall encourage private investment to make up for the NT$391.3 billion shortfall to lessen the government's financial burden.

Of the 632 projects in the Six-Year National Development Plan reviewed, 69 have been completed and 406 are being carried out, 74 are already being planned in detail, and another 30 are on the drawing board. Feasibility studies are being made for 32 projects, while the remaining 21 have not yet been started.

The review has revealed that the supply and demand can be coordinated and balanced. Problems can be resolved and the planned benefits can be realized simply through a comprehensive planning on the use of land, manpower, and material resources.

Transportation construction projects are crucial to national development. Therefore, to realize the goal of developing Taiwan into the transportation hub of the Western-Pacific region, the ROC is completely dedicated to systemizing its international, inter-city, regional, and metropolitan transportation networks. The Mass Rapid Transit System, the Second Freeway, the Taipei-Ilan Highway, and the high-speed railway, which are all actively under construction or planning, will effectively increase transportation capacity in the ROC. Likewise, emphasis has been placed on raising the quality and effectiveness of telecommunications. The government has drafted the *Statutes Governing Incentives for Public Participation in Transportation Projects*. After the statutes   47 pass through legislative procedures, new opportunities will open up for the private sector to participate in transportation development, thereby creating a new environment and expanding the development of transportation networks throughout the ROC.

Developing the Economy

The ROC's economy grew by 6.2 percent in the first half of 1993, and the consumer price index increased by an average of 3.2 percent compared to the same period in 1992, indicating that a stable growth has been sustained. However, the trade surplus dropped by 36.7 percent to US$3.33 billion compared to the same period in 1992. Growth in industrial production was rather low while manufacturing registered almost no growth. Since world economy still shows no sign of recovery, the ROC must rely on increasing domestic demand, especially investment by the private sector, to maintain its economic growth. With this understanding, the executive branch in July of 1993 formulated an "Economic Stimulus Package to Promote Private-sector Investment" and "Measures to Implement the Economic Stimulus Package" for implementation by pertinent government agencies. The chief objective is to "comprehensively promote private investment and generate prospects for economic development."

The government has also set two major policy goals: to speed up the upgrading of industry, and to develop the Taiwan area into an operational and transportation center for the Asia-Pacific region. To accomplish these goals, the government shall adopt the following strategies:

■ Make more effective use of resources by improving the overall investment environment and strengthening market functions, continue such policies as economic liberalization and globalization, facilitate a rational distribution of resources in both the private and public sectors, and attain effective use of resources, beginning with land, manpower, technology and finance.

■ Foster cross-Straits economic and trade development by formulating a clear-cut and pragmatic economic and trade policy based on the principles of market economy and aimed at the complementary utilization of cross-Straits resources and the division of industry.

■ Increase efficiency in government agencies by making reasonable adjustments to government organizational structure, modernizing the civil service system and revising relevant laws and regulations, expediting the policy of privatizing national enterprises and allowing the private sector to compete so that the economy can be thoroughly revamped through the vigor exhibited by private enterprises, and setting up a cabinet-level policy task force to fully coordinate the opinions of various agencies to revive their esprit de corps.

The above strategies should lead to an acceleration of industrial upgrading and improvement of the economic structure over the short term and well into the long term. However, in view of global economic conditions and rapid changes in the development of cross-Straits trade and economic relations, and in consideration of the ROC's domestic economy and its citizenry's desire for change, it is imperative that we keep abreast of the times and adopt holistic long-range plans so as to deal with the changing situation and create prospects for further economic development. Therefore, having considered the pros and cons, we are expediently mapping out a plan to make Taiwan into an operational and transportation center for the Asia-Pacific region, consisting of multi-functional centers for research and development, finance and transportation. Making use of Taiwan's unique location and economic conditions, the government will develop the Taiwan area into a highly open economic entity so that talent, capital, goods and information can flow freely. This should fashion Taiwan into an attractive investment area where capital and talent converge, invigorating the economy and gradually developing Taiwan into an operational and transportation center for the Asia-Pacific region.

In addition, the government has coordinated major cases of private-sector investment since September of 1992 with outstanding results. From January to June of 1993, the government coordinated a total of 229 cases of private investment in the manufacturing sector, each involving over NT$200 million. These projects with an estimated total investment of NT$873.3 billion will be completed between 1993 and 1997.

One important governmental task is to expand international economic and trade relations on all fronts. Special emphasis is being placed on improving Sino-American, Sino-European and Sino-Japanese trade relations. To upgrade the industry and to transform the small and medium-sized manufacturing enterprises, the government is promoting industrial automation, upgrading technology in traditional industries, developing newly-emerging technological industries and products, and assisting small and medium-sized enterprises by bolstering their human resources and replenishing their capital supply.

Sound finance is the pillar of economic development. The government is proceeding in an orderly fashion to establish a "pay for what you get" system in order to foster fairness of financial burdening among citizens. We are also making appropriate use of public bond policies to raise capital for national construction projects, revising laws on revenue and expenditure distribution to shore up the financial condition of local governments, improving the tax system to set up a good taxation environment, reforming tax administration to better serve the public, lowering import tariffs to facilitate clearing goods through customs, and fully enforcing financial liberalization, globalization and discipline.

Agriculture in the ROC is presently at a transitional stage. It will soon evolve from the agricultural mode of a developing nation to that of an economically advanced nation. Adhering to the policy of "developing agriculture, rebuilding farming villages and looking after the livelihood of farmers," the government will continue to implement a comprehensive agricultural adjustment package, pursue such goals as corporatizing agricultural production, modernizing living conditions on farms and naturalizing the farming village ecology. Major efforts taken include: stepping up the management of importing agricultural products, planning and implementing adjustment measures for the agricultural sector in response to our preparations for joining GATT, mapping out the use of agricultural lands in conjunction with the Economic Stimulus Package, improving agricultural production and distribution, creating new agricultural technologies, strengthening farmers' organizations, bolstering ecological preservation, and reconfiguring the structure of fisheries.

Developing Culture, Education, Science and Technology

The functions of education are to pass on the cultural heritage, stimulate thinking and new insight, and nurture talent. Education in the ROC is practically universal in quantitative terms, but still needs further refinement in terms of quality. In the future, the quantitative growth of higher education in the ROC will be adequately controlled, while emphasis will be placed on upgrading the quality of education to cultivate the professional talent needed for national development. At the primary education stage, we shall bolster education about democracy, the rule of law, morality and living. The government will continue to experiment with an examination-free high school admission program, and to make plans for heading toward a ten-year compulsory education standard to develop and improve junior high technical and art training, and will reasonably adjust the tuition structure, so as to balance educational development in urban and rural areas, upgrade the quality of compulsory education, and nurture a modernized citizenry. In addition, the government will promote adult and special education, reconfigure the technical and vocational educational systems, and supervise the sound development of private schools. And under the principles of universal availability and greater sophistication for sports, the government will promote sports and exercise for the entire people, while cultivating and providing incentives for outstanding athletes.

The goals for developing science and technology are to strengthen cooperation in specialized fields and to improve the system of management, to make effective use of scientific and technological resources, upgrade research and development results, and foster integration of up-stream, mid-stream, and down-stream technology. We shall carefully select major innovative technological items or measures and then meticulously plan and promote their research, encourage experiment and practical scientific research, accelerate the cultivation of talent in newly developed high-tech fields. We shall increase investment in basic scientific research, spur on new basic and applied research, and foster harmony between scientific development and a humanistic society. We shall also set up an inter-disciplinary research group system, increase promotion of academic and industrial cooperation, spur the upgrade of industry, promote international large-scale laboratory cooperation, and narrow the gap with advanced nations in scientific and technological capability.

To ensure that all citizens can enjoy a prosperous, yet polite and fun-loving culture and lifestyle, the government is actively promoting various projects for cultural regeneration to improve the literary and artistic environment, foster cultural development, rectify social customs, and upgrade the cultural upbringing of the citizenry. The government will also work for a balanced development of urban and rural culture and promote cross-Straits and international cultural exchanges, so as

53

to mold a modern Chinese culture and consolidate the will of the Chinese people.

Establishing a Harmonious and Peaceful Society

The ultimate goal of governmental administration is to establish a harmonious and peaceful society to provide the citizenry with a fair, just, stable, peaceful, and happy environment for living and growth, so that each member of society can enjoy freedom from want or fear, and can be united within a constitutional system of government to enjoy his rights and fulfill his obligations. To achieve this goal, the government will step up social welfare work in the future and actively carry it out by establishing an order of priority based on such factors as the overall allocation of national resources, social fairness and justice, and the government's financial capability. Specific laws have been formulated to protect the welfare of the aged, children, juveniles, and the disabled. A welfare law for women is also being drafted now. Universal national health insurance is to be implemented as scheduled by the end of 1994. According to statistics, the central government's expenditure for welfare services grew by 14 times, from NT$1.9 billion plus in fiscal 1989 to NT$26.7 billion plus in fiscal 1994. This figure will continue to grow in order to improve welfare measures. Meanwhile, the government is determined to comprehensively track down and eliminate hoodlums and burglars, clean up narcotics, and make great efforts to promote its war on drugs. It will further strengthen public order through the implementation of a police duty district system. It also expects to root out crime through education, publicity, and family channels.

In addition, the government has drafted a plan to safeguard public security. Construction management, fire control, business registration, campus security, labor safety, food sanitation, traffic management, and the management of tourist and recreational facilities will be improved or strengthened. They will be assigned to responsible government agencies for implementation, so as to safeguard the people's lives and assets. Other major tasks will include: enforcing reasonable environmental protection standards, improving the quality of drinking water, properly disposing of garbage, strengthening environmental sanitation, and controlling water, air, and noise pollution; insisting on a fair transaction system for the protection of the rights and interests of consumers; protecting intellectual property rights and rare animals and wildlife for establishing a good national image; emphasizing the rights and interests of laborers, farmers, fishermen, aborigines, and retired servicemen, and improving their living conditions and environment; promoting the development of new cities (towns) and communities; and constructing public housing on a large scale.

Honorable legislators: President Lee Teng-hui once told us that "...the modernization of the nation has a long way to go. Economic development will inevitably bring changes to society and at the same time broaden political participation of the public, speeding up the transformation of the political ecology. We just cannot simply be content with the achievements we now have." I feel deeply convinced of these words. Confronted with the problems resulting from simultaneous and rapid transformation in politics, foreign relations, social affairs,

55

economics, and culture, we must be calm. These problems are the growing pains of national progress and are the necessary price of social development. If we can make sure of our direction, keep our principles, and stand firm, then a challenge will mean an advance, and an effort will bear a new hope. My wisdom might be limited, but the wisdom of the entire citizenry is boundless. The capability of administrative organs might be limited, but the capability of the entire citizenry is beyond limitation. At the juncture when the nation is replacing the old with the new so as to create new chances, I hope you honorable legislators and the entire citizenry will give the administrative branch your comments, strength, and support. Let us jointly establish an honest and efficient administration to generate enough power to develop the economy, extend our foreign relations, maintain social order, promote culture, and reinforce national defense, in hopes that the Republic of China can stand proudly in the Western Pacific, create new horizons for the Chinese people, and make important contributions to the peace and welfare of the Asia-Pacific region!

The premier exchanges views on national affairs with Mrs. Corazon Aquino, former president of the Philippines, during her visit to Taiwan on June 9, 1993.

A Sacred Commitment: To Upgrade the Taiwan Experience toward a Harmonious Society

Address Delivered at the 48th
Taiwan's Retrocession Day Celebration
October 23, 1993

In two days' time, it will be the 48th Taiwan's Retrocession Day. The Republic of China's achievements in the Taiwan area over the past 47 years are known to all. The most open, stable and prosperous living ever witnessed in the history of China that we enjoy today — a result achieved by the entirety of our citizenry — is well worth prizing. Through our struggle of sweat and tears, we have come to realize the truth of the expression, "The harder you sow, the more harvest you will reap." However, at our joyous moment of harvest should we not soberly and wisely ask ourselves what our society still lacks after all this progress and prosperity? Also, what kind of life should we pursue? And what kind of society do we want?

Since I moved from the provincial government to the Executive Yuan, I have often pondered this problem: How can we charter a course for building a harmonious society in the Taiwan area amid the drastic social change, rapid economic development, gradual political liberalization and complete freedom of speech?

If we examine the situation dispassionately, it is not difficult to discover that in our society, though national income is constantly rising and our lives are increasingly improving, materialism becomes the order of the day, weakening human relations. Some people complain that violence prevails, drugs and prostitution are rampant, money games are the rage, and that the weak and disadvantaged do not receive proper care. If these scourges that hinder the progress of our country and society are not removed, they will not only threaten to bedevil our society and people, but also pose as burning problems of government administration.

I have often thought that what the people expect at present is not just economic growth or the accumulation of wealth, but rather a more effective government, a more rational citizenry and a more caring society. The objective of the government's much-emphasized all-round administration is to foster the early realization of the ideal of a harmonious society.

Establishing a harmonious society is an inevitable responsibility of the government and a grand task that the whole citizenry would like to see accomplished. We must pursue this ideal from economic, political, cultural and educational, and social directions.

Economically, we must maintain social prosperity, promote the upgrade of industry, sustain the economic growth, increase employment opportunities and investment so that the citizenry is free from want and that wealth is more equitably distributed.

Politically, we must implement multiparty politics, realize constitutional democracy, improve the practice of elections, strive for a greater maneuvering space in diplomacy, participate in the international community, and raise our national status and dignity.

Culturally and educationally, we must emphasize the teaching of morality, ethics, democracy and the rule of law to our citizenry; increase recreation facilities; beautify the environment; raise the quality of education; promote cultural activities; improve the social mores; reduce the pressure of school entrance exams; develop adult education; and promote sports for the entire populace.

Socially, we must set up a social security system, implement national health insurance, establish a national annuity system, step up relief and aid to the poor and needy, improve law and order, foster community development, protect the weak and disadvantaged groups, and ensure peace and health for our citizenry.

Of course, we understand that a harmonious society is not a task that can be achieved overnight, but is rather a massive social project. However, we can do it if we can persist. To sketch the outlines for such a harmonious society, the government is to assure the citizenry that we are committed to this ideal. Our ultimate goal is to unite the forces of government and the private sector to reach the following ten objectives:

■ To foster caring and mutual assistance, thereby building a harmonious and united society.

■ To promote law abidance and discipline, thereby building a democratic and law-and-order society.

■ To foster balanced development in urban and rural areas, thereby building a well-off and equitably prosperous society.

■ To develop a reasonable living environs, thereby building a comfortable and tidy society.

- To eliminate the influence of privilege and violence, thereby building a fair and just society.

- To eliminate drugs and prostitution, thereby building a healthy and clean society.

- To advocate proper recreation and sports, thereby building a peaceful and content society.

- To encourage active participation by the public, thereby building an outspoken and assertive society.

- To improve cultural development at the grassroots level, thereby building a wealthy yet genteel society.

- To realize social welfare policies, thereby building a warm and mutual-help society.

The ideal of a harmonious society is extraordinarily lofty, and thus not easily accomplished. To realize this ideal, we must strive to:

- Construct a pleasing living space, including such measures as beautifying public buildings, setting aside public areas, constructing urban landscapes, following through building management and public safety, eliminating visual and audio pollution, reducing urban signboard clutter, and balancing urban and rural development. This is the spatial harmony that we must achieve;

- Cultivate a modest and polite national character, including such measures as promoting national etiquette, enforcing living standards, stressing humanistic education, recognizing good deeds and behavior, elevating the level of our media culture, reducing pornography and extravagance, cultivating humane quality, and sponsoring cultural activities. This is interpersonal harmony that we must pursue;

■ Foster traditional benevolent virtues, including such measures as actualizing environmental protection, advocating ecological conservation, establishing the concept of conservation, encouraging community relationships of caring and mutual assistance, rectifying extravagant and wasteful habits and customs, and exalting the virtues of charity for the weak and poor. This is the environmental harmony that we must promote; and

■ Provide the conditions to live peacefully and work contentedly, including such measures as earnestly cleaning up crime, cracking down on hoodlums and thieves, eradicating drugs, tracking down and rescuing adolescent prostitutes, protecting the life and property of each citizen, establishing honest and efficient government, thoroughly carrying forward administrative renovation, promoting welfare policies, and making good use of social resources. This is the social harmony that we must bring into reality.

These four kinds of harmony — spatial, interpersonal, environmental, and social — must be well considered in every respect and linked together in order to attain our ideal of building a harmonious society. I would like to explain here the welfare task that our government should actively promote. Several thousand years ago, Kuan-tzu advanced the concept that "only when people are well fed can they be well bred." Confucius also said that "the aged should live out their lives in a fitting way; the able-bodied should have work; the young should be properly reared; and the widowers, widowed, orphaned, disabled and ill should be cared for." Basically, these concepts are closely related. To use modern political theory to interpret them,

63

we must establish a perfect system of social welfare from the grassroots level on up. This system should at least include:

- A social security system that utilizes vocational training, employment assistance, unemployment insurance, and vocational accident insurance to provide guarantees for the life of the entire citizenry.

- A social insurance system that utilizes universal national health insurance to underwrite the expenses incurred from accidents and to share the burden of health risks, as well as protect those citizens who need special care by means of a system of old age, bereavement, and handicap annuities.

- A social welfare service that provides child welfare, where protection and care are of primary importance; adolescent welfare, where guidance and growth are of primary importance; elderly welfare, where health and pensions are of primary importance; handicapped welfare, where finding employment and care are of primary importance; and women's welfare, where equality and respect are of primary importance.

- Social assistance subsidies that guarantee a basic standard of living for our citizenry through low-income living cost allowances, medical subsidies, accident and emergency assistance, and foster their ability to support themselves by such measures as providing work in place of welfare payments, and start-up business loans, vocational training, and employment counseling.

In addition to making fair and reasonable use of government resources, the social welfare system as a whole shall mobilize the entire power of society to give priority care to the weak. If, instead of engaging in claptrap or playing to the gallery, everyone of us can do his part and give all that he can, then I believe we can contribute to establishing a harmonious society.

The government absolutely has the sincerity and determination to establish a harmonious society and ensure the welfare of the entire populace. However, the government cannot spend at will its limited financial resources, creating an accumulation of debt. This debt, in fact, would become the debt of the entire populace, or even that of subsequent generations. Because the government and society belong to everyone, the intense participation of the private sector is extremely important. Some recent proposals have given too much weight to the role of the government and the responsibility of the nation while failing to factor in the share of individuals, families, and social organizations. In other words, they have overlooked the strength of the private sector.

It has always been the government's nation-building policy to enrich the people. If we overlook the power of mutual assistance in the private sector, we would be too neglectful of the tremendous social vitality stored up in the private sector and squander this valuable resource. I believe that a harmonious society basically means caring and interacting out of love for one another. This sort of society not only redistributes resources, it also enhances human virtues: not only through the welfare administration of the government, but also by expressions of mutual assistance and support among the public. Therefore, in terms of giving full play to the strength of the private sector, "benevolence leading to kindness, and goodwill producing harmony" is the very corner-stone of a harmonious society.

I deeply believe that as long as every one of us can care more about others, try a little harder to do things, and cherish our material possessions more, we can spiritually bolster the development of a harmonious society. There are at least four kinds of private-sector resources which deserve our attention: religious belief, family ethics, voluntary service, and community awareness.

Religion is a major factor of social stability. All religions have prospered in our society because the ROC Constitution protects the freedom of religious belief. The power of religion is very impressive: It makes great contributions in terms of material assistance, spiritual comfort, medical healing, defanging cruelty and violence, cleansing the heart of greed and lust, and increasing the spirit of harmony. The benevolence and righteous deeds of those who are religious often can extend to places where even the power of government cannot reach, making religion an indispensably helpful power in a harmonious society.

Families constitute the roots of a society. Family love and joy, as well as feelings of kinship, are the most binding link in all socially interactive relationships. In a harmonious and happy family, inner peace and self-assurance naturally decrease alienation and indifference, and virtually eliminate crime and unrest. The power of the family not only maintains personal ethics, it also offers a shelter for those who suffer setbacks, and provides a starting point for picking oneself up and getting back into the race. Members of a family are emotionally interdependent and help each other solve many problems. The vitality this brings makes the family the main pillar of a harmonious society.

Like-minded public-interest organizations and voluntary service teams, through their exclusively public-interest objectives, combine the kind-hearted and warm forces of society to allow those with nowhere to turn to receive appropriate care. These groups also hasten the pace of tangible and intangible development in a locality, as well as reduce alienation between members of society and increase mutual trust between people. Voluntary service workers, who give no thought to fame or wealth but rather generate the glow of human nature, are the source of light and catalyst for a harmonious society.

The communal relations produced by living among close neighbors, if properly fostered, can form a sense of communal public interest, allowing residents with highly similar backgrounds to develop a strong bond, foster a common set of values, provide each other with mutual help and protection through thick and thin, and can jointly maintain the living quality of their community, develop community resources, participate in the recreational and educational activities of the community, cultivate a refined upbringing, and make the community clean, green, and beautiful.

If we can give full play to these four private-sector resources, especially if the communal public-interest awareness of a living in a common entity can be developed into the social consciousness of *Gemeinschaft*, our society can definitely attain the realm of "dealing with people politely, living with propriety, enjoying a quality life, treating people honestly, and being part of a loving world and a warm society." At that time, we will be able to apprehend through direct experience that the mutual influence of private-sector power is as inexhaustible as the fountain head of a spring, and in no way inferior to the welfare policies implemented by the government through administrative power.

All of us know that it is not easy to reach the goal of a harmonious society. Nonetheless, I would like to assure you here that this is an absolutely sacred commitment of our government. Looking back at the more than 40 years since Taiwan's retrocession, our citizens in the Taiwan area have experienced many obstacles and challenges. However, we have always overcome our difficulties, turned "impossible" into "possible," and finally created the world-renowned Taiwan experience. Therefore, I am deeply confident that with the potential of the 21 million people on Taiwan, as long as we work together with one heart from the top on down, we can certainly attain outstanding achievements again, and upgrade the Taiwan experience toward a harmonious society. For ourselves and for later generations as well, we should work out a splendid scenario for building a harmonious society characterized by mutual respect, caring, and assistance to become the future we all share.

Premier Lien greets Mr. Laurent Fabius, former prime minister of France, during his visit to Taiwan on November 9, 1993.

The Republic of China: Heading toward the Asia-Pacific Era

Address to the Participants in a Lecture Series on
National Development Hosted by the China Times Express
March 29, 1994

This discourse was originally titled "Mr. Sun Yun-suan and his life" in honor of the senior advisor to the president, Mr. Sun, who was once my supervisor. Although Mr. Sun has modestly asked not to use his name, the genuine purpose of this discourse remains gaining a better understanding through a retrospection of the developmental course of our national economy over recent years to better design our future development strategy. Therefore, I would like to take this rare opportunity to express my highest respect for Mr. Sun, who is present here today, and for his painstaking efforts to develop our nation in the past, as well as for all his remarkable achievements.

Mr. Sun served as ROC premier from 1978 to 1984, a transitional period when the ROC was confronted with great challenges at home and abroad. Under his wise leadership, the ROC overcame difficulties arising from the severance of diplomatic relations between the ROC and the U.S., and laid a sound foundation for today's economic development. At that time, Mr. Sun enthusiastically advocated the liberalization and internationalization of our financial and economic sectors. Furthermore, he favored the idea of building Taiwan into the financial, trade and transshipment center of Asia. In

71

light of the likely impact from the reversion of Hong Kong to mainland China in 1997, Mr. Sun encouraged upgrading our domestic industry in order to alleviate any possible negative effect of mainland economic developments on us. A noted remark made by Mr. Sun in June 1982 merits even more of our attention: "When the political, economic, social and cultural gap between the two sides of the Taiwan Straits is narrowed, that will be the time for China's unification." Mr. Sun's wisdom and foresight deserve our wholehearted respect.

I have served in the Executive Yuan for just over one year and am fully aware of the great responsibility I must shoulder in this phase of national development at the turn of the century. Not a single day passes by that I don't remind myself of my duty in the hope that I can, by building upon the sound foundation laid by the achievements of my predecessors, contribute to the future development of our nation and do my duty for my nation and its entire citizenry. Today, the topic of my address is "The Republic of China: Heading Toward the Asia-Pacific Era," and I shall appreciate your comments on what I have to say.

Welcoming the Arrival of the Asia-Pacific Era

Due to the collapse of the communist bloc in the latter half of the 1980s, the world has moved from U.S.-Soviet superpower standoff toward détente, and international relations have entered a post-Cold War era. Although mankind at present still cannot totally avoid the threat of military proliferation and the shadow cast by regional bloodshed and conflict, the principal guiding force behind rebuilding a new world order has without a doubt changed from ideological confrontation to economic cooperation. In light of this unstoppable trend, world attention has gradually shifted from Europe to the strong economic power and promising prospects of the Asia-Pacific area. At this point, I can't help thinking of what a former U.S. secretary of state, Mr. John Hay, said at the beginning of this century: "The Mediterranean is the sea of the past, the Atlantic is the ocean of the present, and the Pacific will become the ocean of the future."

Security and Cooperation in the Asia-Pacific Region

After the end of World War II, Asia first experienced the Korean War and then the Vietnam War. Although the Cold War has come to an end worldwide and there is no war in this region, the Chinese mainland, North Korea, and Vietnam remain under communist control, and therefore leave us still under the shadow of war.

It is generally held that there are three potential crises facing this region: the cloud of suspicion surrounding North Korea's nuclear weaponry and the threat of a possible second Korean war, disputes over the sovereignty of South Sea islands and regional conflict, and expansion of the Chinese communist armed forces and conflict in the Taiwan Straits.

One sobering fact about these three lurking dangers in regional security is that they are intertwined with the extant communist power in the region, an important problem with which we must actively deal. Furthermore, in light of the developments in today's international situation, traditional measures such as containment or antagonism are no longer ideal counter-

73

measures because the former only leads to isolation while the latter inevitably triggers conflict. We cannot expect the communist regimes of the Asia-Pacific region, spurred by containment or antagonism, to manifest reasonable and peaceful responses to the outside world. Confronted by these communist regimes, the most pressing issue we need to consider is how to encourage the expansion of free-market economics, how to reach a regional consensus on "overall development and collective progress," and how to forgive the past, seek future change, and integrate.

This sort of consideration was the basic point I urged on the Chinese communist regime with my call to "shun the zero sum approach in favor of a win-win solution." Nations around the world have clearly witnessed the confrontation and clashes between the two sides of the Taiwan Straits over the past four decades, and fully understand that the Chinese communists have yet to renounce their hostility toward the ROC. Nevertheless, the ROC has adopted a sincere, open-minded, rational, and pragmatic approach, and has done its utmost to open up a future for positive bi-coastal exchange and reciprocal goodwill. This is in fact the only solution to the China issue; there is no other option.

Furthermore, whether we can establish a consensus on intra-regional cooperation is, of course, crucial to the continued peace and stability of the Asia-Pacific region and its efforts to achieve greater prosperity and progress. The present international community is an aggregate whose constituent parts are more reliant upon each other and more mutually influential than in the past. The era of every-nation-for-itself isolationism has long since become history. No country in the Asia-Pacific region can avoid being harmed by instability in the area, regardless of whether it occurs on the Korean peninsula, in the Taiwan Straits, in the South China Sea, or even on the Chinese mainland. Whether we are able to work together for the sake of peace, stability, and prosperity throughout the region and to share equally in the fruits of regional development depends solely on whether or not we can set aside parochial considerations, each give our all to the common effort, and demonstrate mutual support. Most of all, we, the nations of the Asia-Pacific region, need to work with, rather than against, one another. Due to historical grudges, economic disparities, and cultural differences throughout the Asia-Pacific region, the establishment of this concept of working with one another must await the elimination by every country in the region of concern for parochial interest, a broadening of horizons, and a new understanding of the functions and advantages of "Asia and the Pacific Rim as one" or "Asia and the Pacific Rim as one family."

Of course, cooperation requires that we dispense with mutual exclusion, for only then can we seek what we have in common and use our advantages to compensate for each others' shortcomings. The power of cooperation will always surpass the power of separation. If we continue to discriminate amongst ourselves, participate in cut-throat competition, and exclude each other, then the development of the interests of the whole will be rocky. The secretary-general of ASEAN, Ajit Singh, once noted that, through the implementation of pragmatic policies, ASEAN nations have transformed their region into one of the fastest growing areas of the world. Their unity and accomplishments have made the countries of ASEAN the "best advocates" for peace and development both within and beyond the region. Secretary-General Singh further stated, "From its very inception, ASEAN has not been a military alliance. And, now in this post-Cold War era stressing cooperation over conflict, we are even less likely to develop into one. As we strive for peace and prosperity, ASEAN's guiding principles have always been peaceful coexistence and regional cooperation."

The President of the Republic of China, Lee Teng-hui, has always championed pragmatism and cooperation. Politically, he has advocated unofficial "security dialogues" with "no hypothetical enemy and no exclusion of participating members." Economically, President Lee has proposed a "Flying Geese" formation featuring "vertical division of labor with simultaneous growth." This idea is based on a pragmatic consideration of the benefits for the Asia-Pacific region as a whole and accentuates the importance of cooperation and consensus. It deserves the close attention of leaders in the Asia-Pacific region.

Economic Prowess of the Asia-Pacific Region

As the twentieth century draws to a close, the Asia-Pacific region, which circles the Pacific Basin, has demonstrated a surging economic might that cannot be ignored and which symbolizes the coming of the Asia-Pacific century, as can be seen in some basic facts:

The Asia-Pacific region accounts for 37.8 percent of the world's population. Its aggregate gross national product is 51.7 percent of the world's GNP, and the value of its trade accounts for 40.8 percent of trade worldwide. It is a region of tremendous economic might.

On the eastern side of the Asia-Pacific region are three countries (the United States, Canada, and Mexico) that on January 1 of this year established the North American Free Trade Area. The combined population of these three countries accounts for 6.7 percent of the world's population. Their combined GNP amounts to 29.6 percent of the world's GNP, and the value of their combined trade equals 16.8 percent of trade worldwide. They form the world's largest single economic entity.

On the western side of the Asia-Pacific region is East Asia which comprises Japan, Asia's four little dragons, the Chinese mainland, and the ASEAN countries. Its combined population accounts for 30.8 percent of the world's population. Its combined GNP amounts to 20.7 percent of the world's GNP, and the value of its combined trade equals 22.6 percent of trade worldwide. The development potential of this region is staggering. In recent years, the economic growth rates of most of the countries in the region have put the world to shade, leaving other nations outside the region far behind.

The elevation of the Asia-Pacific region's economic status has shifted the locus of global economic development and has changed the world's view of this area. First, people have become aware that the Asia-Pacific region, East Asia in particular, could become the world's largest consumer market and is now the export market of greatest potential. For this reason, many countries have revamped their policies vis-à-vis the Asia-Pacific region. At the suggestion of Australia, the United States, Canada, Japan and others, the Asia-Pacific Economic Cooperation (APEC) forum was established in November 1989 to proclaim the spirit of liberalized regional integration, to rally Asia-Pacific countries to work together, and promote the economic development of this region. In November 1993, President Clinton of the United States elevated the APEC ministerial meeting to the level of an informal summit of leaders, in a strong bid to expand APEC's functions and thereby integrate the economic might of the Asia-Pacific region and strengthen regional cooperation and consensus.

In fact, during the Group of Seven summit in Tokyo during July of 1993, President Clinton explained the U.S. position: He expressed America's willingness to help set up a new "Pacific community" and affirmed America's intention to become a "full-fledged partner in the process of Asian growth." Thus, one can say that the informal summit held in Seattle last year was the Clinton administration's starting point for bringing the concept of the "Asia-Pacific century" into reality. This is a sign that the United States fully understands that the Asia-Pacific region could gradually replace western Europe as the center of world economic activity.

The Regional Role of the Republic of China

Amidst continuing optimistic economic prospects of the Asia-Pacific region, the ROC must consider how to gear its island economy to the rhythm of that of the Asia-Pacific region and the rest of the world. It is therefore imperative for us to think seriously about the important issue and find a way to guide our economy to the best advantage by synchronizing its development with that of other countries in the region.

The ROC has over the last four decades established close economic and trade relations with other members of the Asia-Pacific region. In 1993, total trade between the ROC and Asia-Pacific economies amounted to US$118.6 billion, representing 77.3 percent of Taiwan's total trade. The ROC's most important trading partners are all APEC member countries, including the U.S., Japan, Hong Kong, the Chinese mainland, and ASEAN countries. The ROC established strong economic and trade ties with the U.S. and Japan as early as the 1950s and 1960s. By the 1970s, the ROC was gradually scouting out Southeast Asia to extend its economic and export activities. After people-to-people exchanges between the two sides of the Straits were allowed in the mid-1980s, the rate of economic and trade exchanges between the Taiwan area and the Chinese mainland began to accelerate. Today, the Chinese mainland and Hong Kong are key export markets, as well as vital trade and economic outposts for the ROC.

The ROC's total overseas investment exceeds an estimated US$20 billion, more than 80 percent of which consists of investment in APEC member countries. In 1993, the ROC's investment in this region comprised more than 90 percent of its total overseas investment. Likewise, most of the investment in Taiwan is made by foreign companies and overseas Chinese from Asia-Pacific nations. In 1993, investment in Taiwan by Asia-Pacific nations amounted to US$980 million, representing 81 percent of the total investment there from abroad.

No matter from which perspective one views the situation, progress and prosperity in the ROC are intimately bound up with the Asia-Pacific region. The developmental goals of the ROC on Taiwan have been, are, and will remain consistent with the developmental goals pursued by all people in the Asia-Pacific region. As an Asia-Pacific country, the ROC cannot and should not place itself outside the integral development of the region.

Establishing the Taiwan Area as an Asia-Pacific Operations Center

We are actively planning to develop the Taiwan area into an Asia-Pacific operations center to strengthen cooperation between the various Asia-Pacific countries as they join hands in the joint pursuit of social well-being. The island of Taiwan is located at the nexus of the Pacific island arc and serves both as a linkage point between Northeast and Southeast Asia and as North America's gateway into Asia. In the past, Taiwan was regarded geopolitically and strategically as "an unsinkable aircraft carrier." Today, in terms of geoeconomical viewpoint, Taiwan can be turned into a "flourishing and convenient operations center."

Even more noteworthy is the fact that the ROC has established a solid manufacturing base and an attractive domestic market, in addition to such positive and beneficial attributes as outstanding domestic business management capability and a manufacturing network. Accordingly, the government in July 1993 announced that while implementing its Economic Stimulus Package, establishment of an Asia-Pacific operations center would be added to its medium- and long-term development goals. The Executive Yuan has already formed a special task force responsible for carrying out this work. International consulting firms have also been commissioned by the Council for Economic Planning and Development (CEPD) to conduct assessments and make plans.

The results of the initial evaluation indicate that the Taiwan area has the potential to be converted into an operations center, including a manufacturing center for the research and development of high-value-added goods, a personnel training center, an administration and management center, a technical assistance center, an air and marine transportation and distribution center, a civil aviation center, an express delivery postal center, a telecommunications center, a media enterprise center, and a financial center. The concept of an operations center fits perfectly with the idea initiated in the early 1980s by Sun Yun-suan, senior advisor to the president, to build Taiwan into the financial, trade, and transportation hub of East Asia.

We can foresee that after completion of planning and evaluation for the Asia-Pacific operations center, the ROC government must persevere with even greater determination and efficiency in carrying out various projects related to transportation, information and broadcasting, cultivation of manpower, upgrading of the manufacturing industry, and research and development in science and technology. This is one of the main reasons for the government to pool its energies and carry out administrative reform. This is also why I have emphasized again and again that administrative reform is a never-ending task. We must modernize, liberalize, and internationalize our system, laws, regulations, and rules. We must also have an administrative system that is thoroughly service-oriented, free of corruption and highly efficient before we can actively develop Taiwan into a thriving and convenient Asia-Pacific operations center.

Some people say that the ROC government's decision to carry out the plans for an Asia-Pacific operations center is based on concerns over the return of Hong Kong to the Chinese communists in 1997. In fact, our thinking on this subject is different. On March 1 of this year, at a legislative hearing, I publicly announced four principles on dealing with the issue of Hong Kong and Macau. The first is to preserve the prosperity, freedom, and democratic system of Hong Kong and Macau. The second is to continue developing our relations with Hong Kong and Macau in a mutually beneficial environment. The third is to respect the wishes of the people of Hong Kong and Macau. The fourth is to define the long-term political identity of Hong Kong and Macau. Our efforts to establish the Asia-Pacific operations center does not conflict with these four principles and is absolutely vital for furthering the development of the ROC on Taiwan. As an Asia-Pacific operations center, the ROC will naturally cooperate with other operations centers in the region to everyone's mutual benefit and complementarity, so as to jointly promote the prosperity of the entire Asia-Pacific region.

The ROC Attaches Great Importance to Its Status among ASEAN Nations

The ROC has consistently set great store by its relations with ASEAN countries. Taiwan businessmen are encouraged to invest in ASEAN countries to strengthen trade relations and economic ties. In fact, there is clearly a high degree of complementarity between Taiwan and ASEAN nations in such production conditions as resources, markets, manpower and land; vast Chinese communities there could strengthen necessary liaison. And especially since ASEAN members in the future will form a free trade area, the early establishment of production bases and outposts in this region by the ROC should be especially advantageous to our overall economic and trade development.

Earlier this year during the week of February 9 to 16, President Lee visited the Philippines, Indonesia, and Thailand, and reached a common understanding with regional leaders on upgrading bilateral economic cooperation, while I made a trip to Malaysia and Singapore between December 31, 1993 and January 5, 1994. Quite evidently, ties between Taiwan and these countries are growing increasingly close. In order to combine forces, jointly strive for growth and progress, and realize the task of economic cooperation among Southeast Asian nations, the Executive Yuan in March of this year instructed the government departments involved to take concrete steps to augment special investment projects. These include joint ventures in the Subic Bay industrial area of the Philippines, joint ventures on Indonesia's Batam Island, investment projects in Singapore and Malaysia, as well as assistance in developing tourism, promoting rural development plans, manpower resource training, and the strengthening of technological and cultural exchanges, as well as the signing of bilateral agreements on the protection of investments and the avoidance of double taxation.

83

We do not intend that the strengthening of our friendship with Southeast Asian countries adversely affect cross-Straits relations. We do not even rule out the possibility of joint ventures with Southeast Asian countries in a third area, including the Chinese mainland. This intention is sufficient to prove that we have consistently displayed a positive attitude that is based on the principles of parity and reciprocity to continually promote beneficial relations between the two sides of the Straits. I long ago once pointed out that instead of accentuating ideological antagonism, the two sides should view their relations from a perspective of rational pragmatism, reciprocal cooperation, and the long-term development of our nation and race. In the last few years, Taiwan and the Chinese mainland have developed increasingly frequent trade relations which have benefited both sides — one kind of "win-win" situation. The ROC government will continue to promote positive relations between the two sides of the Straits. Modifying our Chinese mainland policy when it is appropriate to do so and operating by the market mechanism allows economic development between the two sides of the Straits to be flexible and complementary. A sound industrial division of labor in the area would increase the dimensions of economic growth on the both sides of the Straits.

ROC Determination and Efforts to Pay Back the International Community

Today, as we explore the possibilities of Asia-Pacific cooperation, I still want to stress that for our own survival and growth, we need to open up more room for maneuver in the international community. In terms of both the international arena and the Asia-Pacific region, we will absolutely not change our principle of active participation in international activities and paying back the international community. This isn't a matter of "two Chinas" or "one China, one Taiwan," and is even less something about "Taiwan independence," but rather, is an issue of justice and dignity. We won't, we shouldn't and we can't compromise this stance, just as we cannot budge from democracy and freedom.

The effort to join the United Nations is a long-term struggle, while participation in APEC and GATT is our present focus. Our willingness and contributions to international councils and activities should win wide-spread acknowledgment and support, and thereupon spur our direct contact with member governments and frequent exchanges of high-ranking officials, as well as facilitate solutions to substantive economic problems through multilateral and bilateral negotiations. This should have a positive influence and profound significance for the welfare of the international community as a whole.

Furthermore, in order to repay the international community, the ROC in 1988 set up the International Economic Cooperation and Development Fund to provide financial and technological aid needed by developing countries. About US$300 million in low interest loans had been granted by the end of 1993 to help developing countries engage in the construction of transportation, roadway, water, and community facilities, or for use by small and medium-size enterprises. Nearly half of these loans were to help ASEAN members. We shall continue to fortify the functioning of the fund, assist the economic development of developing nations, and give high priority to the needs of the Asia-Pacific region so as to fulfill our international obligations.

An Indispensable Partner in the Pursuit of Peace, Cooperation, and Prosperity

Ladies and gentlemen: The Asia-Pacific region is now on the threshold of a new era. The continued growth of this region will inevitably make Asia-Pacific countries the economic fulcrum of the world. Nations in the area have to set aside ideological antagonism and jointly explore resources through cooperative means, spur economic integration, do all possible to maintain peace, and create progress and prosperity. Upon his return from a trip to three Southeast Asian nations, President Lee stressed the importance of "peace, cooperation, and prosperity." We are confident that through the joint and pragmatic efforts of all Asia-Pacific countries, ideological antagonism in the region will fade away, creating a new opportunity for peace. The foundation of mutual trust and reciprocity is being improved, leading to unprecedented hope for cooperation. The scale of trade and economic interaction is expanding, serving as a fresh impetus for prosperity. The "Asia-Pacific Century" we are striving to configure should be an era of political trust and reliance, economic reciprocity and mutual benefit, and cultural exchange and enjoyment.

As a member of the Asia-Pacific and international communities, the ROC has made important contributions to the development of this region. We have always adhered to the ideal of "helping and benefiting others as well as ourselves." As we hereafter look to a brand-new "Asia-Pacific Century" brimming with hope, we will more actively develop ourselves and bolster international cooperation, to become an indispensable partner in the pursuit by the Asia-Pacific region of peace, cooperation, and prosperity.

Premier Lien congratulates
President of Honduras Carlos
Roberto Reina at his inaugu-
ration on January 27, 1994.

Beyond the Transitional Period and into the Next Millennium

An Article Appearing in the *United Daily News*
May 2, 1994

Following two catastrophic world wars in the first half of this century, mankind has come to know the joy of peace restored. The recent collapse of the Soviet communist empire has shown that, for the first time in recent memory, we have been able to avert by peaceful means the possible outbreak of a global war and the complete annihilation it would bring. People around the world have thus become more hopeful about the prospects for peace and development.

The Republic of China shares this confidence about the future. Our "Taiwan miracle" has already been hailed worldwide, and we will continue to forge ahead. In particular, we must adapt to a changing world, grasp new opportunities, and succeed in our political, economic and societal transitions so that we can become a modern nation by the turn of the century. In my view, this great effort should be conducted on four major fronts.

Chinese Culture:
Synthesis, Innovation, and Advancement

The concept of culture covers all aspects of man's living conditions, which change as society evolves. Hence,

91

it is not always easy for people to define their own culture and the direction it is heading. Judging by current social trends, we in Taiwan need most to establish a cultural consensus on balanced development, the heightening of ideals, and the promotion of public welfare.

The sustained development of culture is basically non-exclusive. Creative and regenerating forces can be unleashed only through balanced absorption, awareness, and synthesis. While recognizing that we are the inheritors of Chinese culture, we must not overlook the essence of other cultures. While affirming our traditional ethics, we must not disregard modern trends. While keeping up with the cultural mainstream, we must not underestimate the value of ethnic and cultural diversity. Pop culture should be assigned the same value as high culture, because culture uprooted from its soil is destined to wither. All citizens should have a basic understanding of various cultural realms, for with mutual respect and tolerance we can enrich our lives and help promote balanced cultural growth by borrowing from and adding to other cultures.

Culture may be defined on three levels — material or economic, systemic or behavioral, and conceptual or valuational. We have achieved affluence in material terms and have laid a firm foundation in systemic terms. But, much remains to be done on the conceptual and valuational level. Democracy and affluence have confused certain of our values, disrupted the traditional social order and spiritual life in our community, and led to discontent over certain societal phenomena. People cannot help asking themselves when this transitional period, along with the pain it has brought, will end.

In fact, the fundamental value system of Chinese culture has been shaped by Confucianism, Taoism and Buddhism. These teachings instruct us on how to live our lives, enjoy nature, be delivered from pain, and pursue happiness. If we can interpret Confucianism, Taoism, and Buddhism in ways that can be understood by modern man and help him to live his life accordingly, we can develop a healthier lifestyle and value system. This would in turn bring stability to our communities and enhance our spiritual lives. We should bear these objectives in mind as we go about developing our culture.

Although an individual's lifestyle reveals his or her culture, people in countries that have compulsory education systems and a high standard of living pay greater attention to their overall cultural image. The Chinese talk about a "rich and genteel" society which takes in the significance of both individual and society as a whole. As one enjoys the freedoms inherent in an advanced society, one must follow both the letter and the spirit of the law and preserve public order. We need to foster public morality, sponsor public welfare programs, protect our environment, and safeguard the overall image of society. We must not be merely nouveaux riches who strive for personal gain with no regard for the public good. As we approach the 21st century, we must realize that we are part of a "common entity." We must help and support each other in the knowledge that we are all members of the same community and that we are the inheritors of a vast cultural legacy. Only then, can we enter the 21st century with the grace of a highly cultured nation.

International Relations:
Resilience, Adaptability, and Breakthrough

Peace has always been the prime foreign policy objective of the Republic of China. Operating under the principle of "one China, two political entities," we are working to improve the international status of the Republic of China on Taiwan. We do believe that in the post-Cold War international community, our democratic achievements and our economic strength will open many doors for us.

Aside from traditional diplomatic tasks, we must further promote the pragmatic policy of "coordinated development." We will continue to provide economic and technical assistance to the Third World while promoting cooperative relations with advanced countries. We look forward to importing technology and strengthening trading ties with all friendly nations, and we are encouraging private companies from the ROC to invest in foreign lands.

The Asia-Pacific region is working hard to promote cooperation on all levels. ASEAN countries, mainland China, Latin American countries, and South Pacific island countries, all need investment capital, technology transfers, and managerial expertise. We are in a position to meet these needs. Multilateral cooperation in the Asia-Pacific region is a win-win proposition for all. While the Chinese communists have done their best to isolate us from the international community, they will never be able to stop us from contributing to the prosperity, progress, and peace of the Asia-Pacific region. We do believe that our contribution will be judged on its own merit and that we will be able to participate in regional, global, and international forums.

Unless we change the communist China's zero-sum mentality, however, relations between the ROC on Taiwan and the Chinese mainland can never be "win-win," and unification will remain unattainable. The Chinese communists must realize that our attempts to achieve diplomatic breakthroughs are not aimed at them or the unification-independence issue.

A Harmonious Society: Persistence, Promotion, and Promise

Urbanization and industrialization result in the diversification of social groups and a certain degree of alienation followed by the emergence of differing values and a tendency towards individualism. As individuals and families face more pressure, government and private agencies begin to play an increasingly important role. We are in a transitional phase during which traditional societal functions are fading away and new modern urban characteristics and personal ethics have not yet completely emerged.

During this transitional phase, society expects the government to create a more comprehensive system of social welfare. While many have called for the establishment of a harmonious society to resolve the problems associated with alienation, a mind-your-own-business attitude still prevails. Almost everybody wants the government to establish a society of democracy and law, and yet many people break the laws that already exist. Government workers, who are trying their best, find it difficult to satisfy individuals who have no sense of collective identity.

And yet, we are as determined as ever to create a harmonious society. Not only does the government need to bolster its social services and powers of public administration, private citizens also need to learn how to live and work side by side in harmony. By serving the community, private citizens do away with indifference and selfishness and help build a society of mutual concern and mutual respect. We are glad to note that in recent years this spirit of social activism has grown to encompass local communities, the Taiwan area, and other countries. The government should join forces with nongovernmental organizations and individuals to uphold the ethics of social responsibility and public interest, for only then can we end the transitional period and usher in a new era of social harmony.

National Development:
Objectives, Orientations, and Directions

Since the lifting of the Emergency Decree in 1987, the Republic of China has undergone significant social, political, and economic changes. President Lee Teng-hui's quiet revolutions are directing the ROC on Taiwan toward a new era in which sovereignty rests with the people. After the current phase of constitutional amendment is completed, the citizens of the Republic of China in the Taiwan area will be able to directly elect the president. The public consensus derived from the election will allow the people — regardless of age, gender, and geography — to form a new common entity. As the next century approaches, we should be thinking about how we can use this opportunity to benefit all Chinese people everywhere.

Taiwan's experience over the past half century has shown that democracy and economic liberalization are the dynamos of national development. Stable, rational and peaceful cross-Straits relations provide a basis from which we can make great strides forward. As a Chinese proverb notes, "A journey of one thousand miles starts with the first step." We should use Taiwan's experience to help all Chinese modernize. Politically, we should continue pursuing reform and establish a thoroughly honest and intelligent government. Economically, we should continue liberalizing and internationalizing our markets, promoting comprehensive development, and building Taiwan into an Asia-Pacific operations center. As for cross-Straits relations, we should stick as close as we can to the *Guidelines for National Unification.* Although the Qiandao Lake tragedy has caused us to stop and reflect upon the great differences between the Chinese communists and ourselves, we still hope the unfortunate incident will not hinder the long-term development of cross-Straits relations. The two sides should continue to allow friendly exchanges, to deal with each other, and to avoid any incident that may have a negative impact.

The development of this nation hinges upon the promotion of a new way of thinking among our people. The same held true for the Renaissance, the Industrial Revolution and the Meiji Restoration. Taiwan's development experience will add new impetus to our long-standing traditions and help us reach a new pinnacle of success. Chinese people in Taiwan should be aware that they are responsible for creating their own cultural renaissance that will lead to a balanced and harmonious time in the history of Chinese culture.

Looking back over the rapid changes that have occurred in the ROC on Taiwan over the past six or seven years, we find that growing social diversity has allowed our people to experience unprecedented democracy and prosperity. While people's values have changed, the ultimate objective, national development, has remained unaltered. We believe that democracy and the will of the people will forge a new common entity in Taiwan of the Republic of China and that the ROC will be a modern nation with freedom, democracy, and an equitable distribution of wealth.

Conclusion

The Republic of China on Taiwan has changed rapidly over the past several years. A peaceful process of constitutional reform has shown the government's determination to promote democracy and enabled us to catch up with Western countries. Likewise, liberalization and internationalization of our economy has brought stability to the Taiwan area. Our substantive economic strength and our desire and ability to reward the international community for running the blockade thrown up by the Chinese communists has allowed us to re-take our position on the international stage under circumstances of extreme difficulty. The gradual implementation of social welfare policies in the name of justice and fairness has promoted social stability and harmony. And, we have had some success in revitalizing our traditional culture, forming national and community identities, pre-

serving our cultural heritage, developing cultural enterprises, and promoting cross-Straits and international
cultural exchanges.

Rapid social changes, though, has brought its share
of problems. We still must balance democracy with the
rule of law, economy with culture, fairness with efficiency, and environmental protection with economic
development. Our main objectives are national unification and modernization. We must not only sustain our
current achievements but also overcome the obstacles of
the transitional period, for only then can we enter the
new millennium with the grace and dignity of a highly
cultured nation.

II. On the U.N. Issue

Premier Lien engages in a friendly chat with President of Dominica Mary Eugenia Charles on February 15, 1994.

"Believe in What You Do; Do What You Believe in" —
The Republic of China's Drive for International Recognition

Address to the 85th Annual Convention of
the Rotary International
June 12, 1994

Since your founding in 1905, you have been committed to the "ideal of service." In fact, although it has gone through several revisions, the basic "ideal of service" has from the start been your goal. Through your four avenues of service — club, vocational, community and international — you have spread the name of your organization and its ideal worldwide.

Your motto, "Service Above Self," expresses the ultimate ideal that humans should uphold during their sojourn on this earth. It is a role model advocated by all the great religions of the world.

As a compliment to your organization, I have chosen your president's theme for this year — "Believe in What You Do — Do What You Believe in" — as the subject of my talk this evening. I would like to take your theme and apply it to the efforts of our nation to expand international contact. Our principal goal is to participate in the United Nations. This cause is supported by an overwhelming majority of our citizens — we believe in it; and we will persevere in the face of strong opposition and obstruction from mainland China against us — we will do what we believe in.

After presenting you with some background information, I will take your 4-Way Test and apply it to our drive for wider recognition. This exercise should help you judge the validity of our cause.

The ROC's Drive for International Recognition

To put in perspective our drive for international recognition, I need to spend a few minutes telling you about the history of the Republic of China since the end of the Second World War. After successfully defeating the Japanese, the Republic of China joined with other Allied nations in San Francisco in 1945 to establish the United Nations. And in 1949, a struggle between communist and democratic forces in China came to a head, and the ROC government moved its headquarters to Taiwan. Since 1949, the mainland has been controlled by the communist government while Taiwan and its adjoining islands have been governed by the ROC government. Both sides of the Taiwan Straits still believe in the ideal of "one China" and are convinced that China will one day be unified. China's history, however, is replete with periods of both union and disunion. So this short forty-some years of separation is not particularly spectacular in the history of our nation. Nevertheless, our ideal of "one China" should not obscure the fact that today there actually exist two political entities on the two sides of the Taiwan Straits.

The enmity between the governments on the two sides of the Taiwan Straits was especially bitter in the first few years following 1949. We were both fighting for world recognition of the justice of our cause. Our differences were heightened when the United Nations voted to give the China seat to communist China in 1971. At that time, friends of the ROC advised us that dual representation might be a reasonable solution, but psychologically we could not accept a compromise that we felt would be a denial of our integrity. Unfortunately, size and population won over and the Republic of China was forced to withdraw from the United Nations it had helped to establish in 1945.

Since 1971, the Republic of China has essentially been isolated in the international diplomatic community. Some of our closest friends and allies are reduced to referring to our country as "people" rather than a state, ludicrous as it may sound. I am personally convinced that some nations were relieved to detach themselves from the midst of the conflict between the two Chinese groups. Both sides' insistence that a decision be made as to who should represent the non-existent "one China" gave other nations the perfect out. And we went along with it, agreeing that it was a Chinese problem to be solved by the Chinese.

Exclusion from the world's councils affected us very badly. In spite of the slight, we labored on and became the 14th largest trading nation in the world, the sixth largest trading partner of the United States, and the holder of one of the largest foreign exchange reserves in the world. We have also been undergoing a bloodless political revolution toward establishing full democracy for our people. But still, we realized that there was something missing. Having become a prosperous nation, we felt an obligation toward other countries and peoples. We wished to help but were prevented from sharing our economic strength and ideals of freedom by our exclusion from the international community. We also want to eliminate the threat of communist domination by our brothers and sisters across the Taiwan Straits. In today's world where technology has practically removed distances between nations, we understood that continued isolation was not only inadvisable but also dangerous.

The drive to gain international recognition began under the leadership of the late President Chiang Ching-kuo and has been accelerated under that of President Lee Teng-hui. It started with the realization that the Republic of China must be pragmatic. Insofar as foreign relations were concerned, it began with an honest appraisal of where we stood and of how to make the most of our situation.

The fact is that 29 nations maintain full diplomatic relations with our country. While observing the obligations and enjoying the benefits of these formal relations, we also understand that we have many substantive, if not political, relationships with a much larger group of nations. These less formal relationships are of several types: economic, cultural, scientific and philanthropic. Despite the lack of formal diplomatic ties, a great many countries gradually acknowledge the necessity of contacts with us. At present, we have 124 representative offices throughout the world.

We, therefore, accepted the de facto situation and began to work from there. Many of you may be familiar with our increasing efforts to gain entrance into international forums. We often have had to use other than our formal name to effect entry because that is part of being pragmatic. We have in the last two years become a full member of the Asia-Pacific Economic Cooperation forum. Our application for accession into the General Agreement on Tariffs and Trade is now being examined and we hope to be admitted by the end of this year. Last September, seven friendly nations from Central America tried to get the United Nations to appoint a committee to study our case. Although the effort did not succeed, we will not be deterred; we are used to fighting for what we believe in.

Most nations would welcome our efforts to play a role in the international community if it were not for their fear of offending mainland China. Let's face it. We conduct ourselves according to international standards: the Republic of China has no human rights problems, we don't export foods made by prison labor, we don't sell nuclear technology to the enemies of the free world, and we have done our best to comply with all international trade covenants. Nonetheless, we remain isolated internationally. Without obstruction from mainland China, the ROC on Taiwan would be able to join most international organizations.

But, as I have said, we are pragmatic. We recognize the problem and are systematically taking steps to solve the problem. We have begun a series of unofficial negotiations with representatives of the Association for Relations Across the Taiwan Straits of mainland China. We hope that in time we can convince them that, during the interlude to eventual unification, our participation in international bodies will contribute to that final goal. Meanwhile, we hope to encourage the mainland to become more free, democratic and concerned about the equitable distribution of wealth among people on the mainland. It is only under such principles that the Republic of China can ever agree to the reunification of our two territories. We will not sell our people to the servitude of dictatorial rulers.

In the meantime, we will continue to enlist the support of more freedom-loving countries for our efforts to become a full-fledged participant in the United Nations.

Applying Rotary's 4-Way Test to the ROC's Drive for International Recognition

Herbert J. Taylor, who became president of Rotary International in 1954, proposed a way for Rotarians to weave the objectives of Rotary International into their personal lives in 1932. The 4-Way Test was adopted by Rotary International in 1943. As all of you know, four simple but profound questions are to be asked when considering an undertaking. If the answer to each question is positive, then the endeavor is worthy of being included in a Rotarian's daily life.

I would like to take the liberty of putting our country's drive to become a full member of the international community to the Rotary's 4-Way Test.

The first test is "Is it the truth?" In other words, does the Republic of China on Taiwan meet the requirement of statehood embodied in the United Nations Charter? Or, is its claim to participate a fraud?

The Republic of China on Taiwan fulfills all of the requirements of statehood; it has territory, people, government, and the capacity to enter into relations with other states. It has all the accouterments of statehood but yet is denied formal recognition as a state by many nations. This is due to an irrational fear of offending mainland China.

Acknowledging the truth of the ROC's existence and according it participation in the world's premier coalition of nations would be acknowledging a fact — a truth. Perpetuating the image of the ROC as a part of the regime on the mainland is a political fiction and as far from the truth as you can get.

The second question is "Is it fair to all concerned?" Not to allow the ROC to participate in the community of nations is exceedingly unfair — a grave injustice to the ROC and its 21 million free people. The ROC has no intention of using its participation to harm any member, even the mainland Chinese regime. We recognize its existence and have no ulterior plan to challenge its membership in the U.N. or in the world community in any way. We are only asking for fair treatment. Until our appeal is seriously considered, the fairness of the U.N. is in serious jeopardy. To be a true and fair body representing the nations of the world, the U.N. is obligated to accommodate a peace-loving state that is willing to carry out the obligations stipulated in the Charter of the United Nations.

The third question is "Will it build goodwill and better friendship?" Building goodwill and better friendship are impossible to come by through exclusion. You do not make a friend of, or display goodwill toward, a person by refusing to allow the person to participate in your organization. "Ill will," not "goodwill," is displayed by refusing to consider membership of a nation qualified to enter the United Nations. The Republic of China has always displayed goodwill and friendship in its dealings with the international community. It is true that we oppose communist regimes. Firstly, we know from experience the havoc such governments can wreak on the lives of human beings who are born to be free. But political conformity is no longer a criterion for participation in the U.N. Secondly, we also recognize that a communist regime exists on the Chinese mainland and have accepted its existence until the people themselves decide or are able to change the situation. Thirdly, we do not approve of the government on the mainland, but we have not given up the hope that it can be led to reform through interactions with us. We are not practitioners of ill will and unfriendliness; we urge, instead, the exact opposite approach.

Finally, "will" acceptance of the Republic of China by the United Nations "be beneficial to all concerned?" Throughout my address, I have tried to answer this question, but let me once again emphasize the benefits of the ROC's participation in the United Nations. The ROC, of course, would benefit tremendously by being able to take part in the decision-making process that affect it on a daily basis. Having a forum in which to voice our concerns would restore the faith of our people in their personal and national worth and remove the stigma that prevents them from participating as equal citizens in the world. Diplomatic isolation has imposed hardships and humiliation on the ROC that no nation or people should be forced to endure.

Not only the ROC, however, would benefit. The international community would also derive distinct advantages from including us in the world body. We have undergone two quiet revolutions — an economic miracle and a bloodless political transformation — experiences of which should be shared with the developing nations of the world on an open and intimate basis. Only through our participation in the United Nations, the political recognition of our existence, can such exchanges be made possible. Our country also has a desire to share its wealth of financial, political, economic and philanthropic achievements with others. When calamity strikes other nations, we are anxious to do our share. We have made many unilateral contributions but have been kept from doing more because of our exclusion from the U.N. Our presence in that organization would open up storehouses that have essentially been closed for too long. Only benefits would come from our participation in the United Nations.

During his visit to Singapore on January 3, 1994, Premier Lien (left) takes time out of his tight schedule to have an afternoon of golf with Interior Minister Wong Kan Seng of the host country.

The Republic of China and the United Nations

An Article Appearing in the *Strategic Review* Quarterly,
United States
July 1994

Despite the end of the Cold War, Asia still faces security concerns. Asian leaders acknowledge that the best way to manage these concerns is through multilateral instrumentalities such as the Asia-Pacific Economic Co-operation forum and the United Nations. While both mainland China and the Republic of China on Taiwan are members of the former, the ROC is excluded from the latter, depriving the U.N. of an important and powerful regional player. The exclusion of the ROC from the U.N. no longer serves any purpose, strategic or otherwise. Indeed, participation by the ROC would contribute substantially to the effectiveness of the world body, especially in Asia.

For all the speculations of journalists and lucubrations of academics, the outlines of what could pass as the architecture of the post-Cold War world have yet to emerge. That having been granted, some common themes about that world recur in the discussions of those who share policy responsibilities.

All the major political players in the Pacific community, for example, ranging from the United States to Indonesia, have expressed an interest in developing a multilateral mechanism for the current and future abatement of growing economic, political and security concerns. Significant trade imbalances, uncertain, if explosive, economic growth and development, the accelerating increase in military inventories, and the emergence of destabilizing political changes in a variety of subregions, all contribute to the real and potential disquiet that troubles the political leadership of the international and regional communities.

In the half century since the end of the Second World War, the United States served as leader of a community of nations committed to peace, stability and economic development. The price paid by the U.S. in that enterprise was heavy both in terms of lives and wealth. In the course of that arduous half-century, Japan, the Republic of Korea and the Republic of China (ROC) on Taiwan, all achieved a rate of material growth and development that made them individually and collectively the envy of the economically less-developed portions of the world community. As the Cold War drew to its close, the nations of Southeast Asia undertook a similar trajectory of remarkable growth. At the same time, the Chinese mainland emerged as an expanding economy with a potential that has implications for the economy of the entire globe.

The rapidly expanding economies of Asia, led by Japan and four newly industrialized countries, including the Republic of China on Taiwan, now produce as much as either the United States or Europe. Even without Japan, steel consumption in Asia is today higher than in the United States or the European community. In bulk, air freight and container cargo already exceed that of the United States and Europe. By the turn of the century,

Asia will account for one-third of the forecast growth for the planet. Today, East Asia provides the United States with an opportunity to exchange US$360 billion in total trade, and a market for more than US$132 billion in exports. More than 2.6 million American jobs depend on the continued availability of East Asian export markets. In an increasingly interdependent economic community, maintenance of peace, stability and prosperity in Asia has achieved critical significance.

Asia after the Cold War

Although Asia is less threatened today by superpower rivalry than in the past, there are still major concerns, such as the military build-up in the region. North Korea has stubbornly resisted international inspection on its major nuclear facilities, feeding the growing belief that it is bent on the development of nuclear weapons. Chinese mainland authorities have recalcitrantly refused to renounce the use of force against the Republic of China on Taiwan. Peking has greatly increased its military budget and bought long-range jets and other sophisticated weapons from Russia, now giving it the ability to project force far beyond its borders and unnerving its neighboring nations.

Furthermore, almost everywhere in Asia there are potential territorial disputes as well as competing claims to offshore islands, adjacent seabed extensions, and exclusive economic zones. For example, there are conflicting claims to the islets, atolls and reefs of the South China Sea, with the ROC, mainland China, Malaysia, Vietnam and the Philippines deploying military garrisons on some of them. While the ROC has proposed

119

setting aside issues of sovereignty over the South China Sea islets to jointly develop the natural resources there for the benefit of all, this proposal has elicited no response so far.

These potential territorial conflicts are compounded by trade tensions. There is friction between Japan and its regional neighbors over trade, technology transfer and resource exploitation. Environmental and drug trafficking concerns only add to the real and potential difficulties. All these sources of tension have provoked vigorous discussion over how best to negotiate the difficulties that will settle on the members of the Asia-Pacific region in the near future.

One suggestion by President Lee Teng-hui of the Republic of China in September 1991 was to urge the nations of the region to uphold the principles of respect for democracy and human rights, including redefining the concept of sovereignty; replacing military force with negotiation and abandoning war as a means of resolving international disputes; promoting market economics through a mixed economic system; strengthening the collective security system that includes regional organizations and the United Nations; and promoting the concept of an organismic community, which he calls *gemeinshchaft*, to jointly tackle the problems of the global village.

The ROC government envisions massive investment by ROC nationals in Southeast Asian nations, including the development of Subic Bay in the Philippines. As recently as February this year, President Lee led a large contingent of ROC government officials, including Foreign Minister Fredrick F. Chien, and business leaders, on a fact-finding tour of the Philippines, Indonesia and Thailand. Besides meeting with the government leaders and economic planners of these nations, he talked with workers and farmers to find out their real needs.

Creating Multilateral Institutions

Government leaders of other countries in the Asia-Pacific region have also acknowledged the need to create multilateral instrumentalities to address regional problems. One of the most noteworthy schemes so far is the Asia-Pacific Economic Cooperation (APEC) forum. In the name of APEC, President Clinton invited Asia-Pacific leaders to a summit meeting following its ministerial session held in Seattle during November 1993. Another summit of leaders from APEC member nations is scheduled to be held in Indonesia this year, adding further significance to the regional organization.

One obvious reason for selecting APEC is its essentially nonexclusive membership policy. Unlike other regional organizations, both the ROC on Taiwan and the Chinese mainland on the other side of the Taiwan Straits are APEC members. Some years ago, Australia urged Asian nations to put together just such an inclusive institutional framework capable of addressing the economic, political and security issues emerging with the conclusion of the Cold War.

The reason for advocating nonprejudicial entry criteria for such an organization is clearly predicated on the recognition that if such a regional arrangement is to provide a forum for the multilateral resolution of "intractable" problems, it is essential that all parties in- *121* volved be afforded an equal opportunity to address proposed solutions. Both good sense and public morality recommend that all communities along the Pacific rim be accorded access to those organizations proposed now for the resolution of regional concerns. In this respect, Australia has argued that any effective regional association in the Asia-Pacific region must ultimately include all countries in the area, including the Socialist Republic of Vietnam and the Democratic People's Republic of Korea. Neither ideological differences, alternative political or economic systems, nor distinct security concerns should be grounds for exclusion from membership.

The logic of this posture is eminently clear. If the issues facing the Asia-Pacific community are as complex as all are prepared to admit, any serious attempt at the resolution of these problems must necessarily involve the participation of all parties concerned. This is particularly true when the potential participants are communities that are critically important to the economic and political development of the entire region. APEC's potential, for example, would be significantly diminished were the Republic of China on Taiwan excluded from its membership. The ROC maintains substantive relations with over 150 nations in the international community, is a leading investor throughout Southeast Asia and the Chinese mainland, is the 14th largest trading economy in the world, the sixth largest trading partner of the United States, characterized by the 25th highest per capita income among all the globe's populations, and the possessor of the second largest foreign exchange reserves in the world. Accordingly, the ROC is an indispensable member of international organizations like APEC, of which it has been a member since 1991.

Since the end of the Cold War, it is apparent that multilateralism is increasingly the principle governing the alignment of Asia's economic, political and strategic relations. Accompanying the growth of multilateralism has been the advocacy of universal inclusion in any of the organizations that are to address regional issues.

The New Importance of the U.N.

If this is true of developments in Asia, there is considerable evidence to suggest that the world community of nations would be responding in much the same fashion to a similar set of international influences. In the immediate past, the United Nations has been called upon to undertake singular responsibilities. In a manner unlike anything in the past, the U.N. has assumed major responsibilities in the Horn of Africa and in concluding the civil strife of the former Yugoslavia.

Changes are also apparent in the United States, where a March 1991 *Time* magazine opinion poll found that 80 percent of Americans favor assigning peace-keeping responsibilities to the United Nations rather than have them undertaken by the armed forces of the United States. This change in attitude has had its effect upon recent American foreign policy. Washington's unprecedented endorsement of APEC as a forum for the multilateral consideration of political, economic and security problems in Asia seems to express an increasing degree of American interest in the collective resolution of issues. More than that, the United States has made recourse to the instrumentalities of the United Nations in its efforts in Somalia and Bosnia. The appeal to the United Nations demonstrates an investment in multilateralism rarely witnessed in the history of American foreign policy.

Like their counterparts in the Asia-Pacific area, many nations of the international community seem to share the U.S. disposition to appeal to multilateralism as a principle in the search for solutions to complex problems. Thus, the United Nations is APEC writ large. What APEC is expected to accomplish for the Asia-Pacific region, the United Nations is expected to accomplish for the world community.

If this is the case, the same logic urging support for APEC would also argue for the support of an expanded role for the United Nations. If the U.N. is to assume unprecedented responsibilities for resolving the many pressing problems that confront the international community, the same recommendation of universal inclusiveness urges itself upon its advocates.

The complexity and intractability of global problems mirror the features of the problems facing the Asia-Pacific region and require the full participation of all those political players whose interests are directly or indirectly involved. The absence of the Republic of China from the membership lists of the world organization is a threat to that organization's capacity for success. By any rational standard, the ROC is a powerful and important entity entitled to representation in the world body.

The United Nations and the ROC

Calls for ROC participation in the U.N. date from the beginning of the 1990s when it became evident to the leadership of the Republic of China that circumstances governing international affairs had radically altered. President Lee Teng-hui charged the relevant national ministries to explore the issue of the ROC's full participation in the United Nations. An effort was mounted to provide the 21 million citizens of the ROC with the representation in the international body to which their fundamental human rights entitle them.

The Republic of China was an original member of the United Nations upon the founding of that body at the conclusion of the Second World War. The ROC assisted in formulating the Charter of the world organization and was instrumental in articulating the Conventions that made fundamental human rights the subject of international jurisprudence.

In the 1950s and 1960s, the rigid bipolarity of the international community assured the Republic of China of U.S. support. The ROC was an important ally to the anti-communist coalition marshaled to contain the expansion of revolutionary Marxism throughout Asia. The support of the ROC in the conflicts on the Korean peninsula and in Southeast Asia was a matter of no small consequence. Allegiance to the ROC led tens of millions of Chinese expatriates in various countries to join the anti-communist cause instead of serving as a fifth column.

By the mid-1960s, however, the intensifying Sino-Soviet dispute became increasingly significant: The international community was no longer overwhelmingly bipolar in terms of power alignments. The fracture of communism along a Chinese-Russian communist fault-line tempted Western nations to flirt with Peking in order to oppose Moscow. At that point, the Chinese mainland's entry into the United Nations became an issue of concern. "For the good of the greater community," it was argued, the Chinese mainland should be allowed "to break out of its isolation" and be drawn into a relationship with the anti-Soviet coalition.

The situation ultimately came down to a choice between the continued presence of the ROC in the world body and the entrance of the Chinese mainland. In October 1971, the General Assembly of the United Nations, with the acquiescence of the United States, voted to transfer the "Chinese seat" from the ROC to the Chinese mainland and the ROC lost its membership. By that time, the mainland had come to be considered an informal "ally" of the United States. To serve the economic, political and security interests of the larger community required sacrificing the immediate interests of the Republic of China on Taiwan.

Those days, however, are over and the situation has changed. In the 1990s, the world is no longer geopolitically bipolar. Further sacrifice of the ROC no longer serves any purpose. Both the Chinese mainland and the Republic of China are members of the world community of nations, and both should be represented in the United Nations.

ROC and Mainland China

Today, little hostility separates the Republic of China from its mainland counterpart. Taipei has rejected the use of force in resolving its differences with Peking. In the ROC, the Chinese communists on the mainland are no longer considered "rebels." The communist regime is now regarded as a political entity ruling the mainland.

Cross-Straits relations improved markedly following the ROC softening of its policy toward the mainland: Taiwan business people are among the heaviest investors in the mainland. Millions of ROC citizens have visited the mainland over the past several years. ROC legislation permits Chinese mainland citizens to visit Taiwan for family reunions. Mainland scholars are invited to attend symposiums in Taiwan and mainland artists are allowed to perform in Taiwan without restrictions. This past March, a big exhibition of books published on the mainland was held in Taipei, with attendance in the tens of thousands.

However, the increasing contact between the two sides of the Taiwan Straits has led to new problems, including fishery disputes, smuggling of human and commercial cargo, crimes against tourists from Taiwan, and hijacking of aircraft from the mainland to Taiwan. The need to solve these problems prompted the establishment of intermediary organizations first in Taiwan and later, on the mainland. The organization representing Taiwan is called the Straits Exchange Foundation, or SEF, for short. Its counterpart on the mainland is the Association for Relations Across the Taiwan Straits (ARATS).

The chairmen of the two semi-official organizations met for the first time in Singapore last year and signed four agreements. Following that, several lower-level meetings were held in Peking and Taipei during which representatives of the two organizations talked and talked, but with little result, mainly because the Chinese mainland authorities refused to recognize the ROC as a political entity even though the ROC recognized the mainland regime as such long ago. In a futile attempt to rewrite history, Peking is trying to gloss over the reality that Taiwan has been a sovereign part of the Republic of China without interruption for more than four decades and that the tentacles of communist rule have never extended as far as the island for even a single moment. This outdated policy of obstreperousness on the part of the Chinese communists is a major block to the ROC's participation in the United Nations.

The fact is, however, that whatever reasons that may have justified the sacrifice of the ROC on the altar of international currying to Peking's hegemonic ambitions in the early 1970s no longer exist. The exclusion of the ROC from the United Nations not only no longer serves any purpose, strategic or otherwise. On the contrary, its participation would in fact contribute substantially to the world body.

The ROC and "the Real Chinese Revolution"

On September 2, 1993, the *Far Eastern Economic Review* identified the Republic of China on Taiwan with "the real Chinese Revolution." The magazine lauded Taiwan as having achieved "a prosperous, self-ruling Chinese society advancing rapidly toward liberal democracy" — an accomplishment envied by most of the world's less developed communities. As a member of the U.N., the ROC could most effectively share with others its experience in economic development and political democratization. In the wake of its explosive economic growth over the past decade or so, the ROC has witnessed a series of quiet revolutions. Power has changed hands and a new legislature has been re-elected. Unlike in most developing nations, these revolutions have occurred without shedding a drop of blood. More profound democratic changes are on the way, as the governor of Taiwan and the mayors of Taiwan's two largest municipal jurisdictions, Taipei and Kaohsiung, also are scheduled to be elected by the end of this year.

Recently, the World Bank attempted to understand what developmental strategies employed by Asia's most rapidly growing and modernizing economies might be transferable to other developing states. The study is flawed because it contains no data from the Republic of China. This might not be the World Bank's fault because the ROC lacks membership in the United Nations, its performance cannot be fully assessed or adequately reported. Data from the ROC are either absent or incomplete in the official reports of the U.N. and its subsidiary organizations. Thus, insights are lost and conclusions weakened by reliance on incomplete data.

Over time, the Republic of China has given ample evidence of a disposition to actively contribute to the humanitarian, economic and cultural activities of the world community. Over the past decade, the ROC has emerged as a major donor of international aid and material assistance. As early as 1980, the ROC provided financial support for the Disaster Relief Aid Fund. In 1988, the ROC established the International Economic Cooperation and Development Fund — and over the years, 43 technical cooperation teams from the ROC have contributed to the development of 31 countries. The efforts of the ROC have been hampered only by its lack of membership in the U.N. Following the devastation of the Gulf War, as a case in point, the ROC was prepared to extend economic aid to some countries ravaged by the war. Its efforts were thwarted by the fact that it is not a member of the United Nations.

Taiwan: Too Big to Ignore

Two decades ago, when the entry of the Chinese mainland into the world organization was advocated, a major argument was that "reality not be ignored." Mainland China was far too "real" to be neglected. Today, no less can be said of the ROC. On November 10, 1990, the *New York Times* editorialized that "Taiwan" was "too big to ignore." That is even more true today than it was in 1990.

Of course, far more fundamental interests are at stake in the exclusion of the ROC from full participation in the activities of the international organization. Everything from cooperation in addressing regional and global environmental threats to the resolution of international conflicts requires the universal and unrestricted participation of all parties whose interests are directly or tangentially involved in the process. Without active global cooperation, the ability of humankind to resolve its most urgent problems will be compromised. Everything recommends that the United Nations, as the world's foremost international authority, abide by its own principle of universality of membership.

Beyond all that, there is a certain irony in the fact that the Republic of China, having served as a founder of the United Nations, and having been instrumental in the formulation of its Charter and human rights Conventions, should find its political, social and economic rights jeopardized by the actions of the United Nations itself.

The preamble of the U.N. Charter contains an affirmation by the signatories of their "...faith in fundamental human rights, [and]...in the equal rights of...nations large and small." The nation was recognized as the agency through which the international community was understood to have transferred rights to individuals. Without representation in the world body, those rights, in a critical and comprehensible sense, are threatened. Without representation in the United Nations, the citizens of the ROC, in general, are denied the right to participate in deliberations that could very well affect their fundamental social, economic and security interests.

The fact that the ROC is not represented in the forums of United Nations has led to discrimination against its nationals when traveling abroad. This denies the fundamental right of nationality to citizens of a community more substantial in terms of population and economic power than two-thirds of the present member nations and territories of the United Nations.

In the world of the mid-1990s there are no longer any reasons, practical or moral, to continue to deny the Republic of China a place in the United Nations. Only the objections of the Chinese communist regime on the mainland hinder an ROC presence in the United Nations.

For two decades, the Peking authorities have stubbornly resisted the ROC's participation in the United Nations and its constituent organizations. The central argument has been that any such participation would establish an independent international personality for the ROC and thereby foster the permanent division of China. Why Peking imagines that this should be the case is unclear, but many nations apparently fear Peking's retaliation and have chosen not to challenge the leadership on the Chinese mainland.

Enhancing Prospects for Chinese Unification

The people and the leadership of the ROC are convinced that reality will eventually persuade Peking to withdraw its objections to the full participation of the ROC in the international community. There is no credible evidence that ROC participation would do anything to impair the prospects of the ultimate reunification of China.

In fact, experience would suggest the contrary. In 1973, both East and West Germany entered the United Nations as full participants. The Marxist German Democratic Republic and the Federal Republic of Germany normalized their relations with the Treaty of December 1973. This dual membership arrangement did not inhibit the ultimate reunification of the German nation divided since the Second World War. Similarly, in the fall of 1991, North and South Korea simultaneously entered the United Nations as full participants. Neither Pyongyang nor Seoul has expressed any fears that this would obstruct the ultimate reunification of the Korean peninsula.

A case could be made that the full representation of all of China in the U.N. would foster, rather than retard, reunification by enhancing contact and interaction between Taiwan and the mainland in the neutral environment of international forums. Contact between Taiwan and the mainland in circumstances of equity and mutual regard could only solidify the foundation upon which a united, democratic and prosperous China might be built.

In this sense, the people and the political leadership of the Republic of China are obligated to pursue those rights available to them as members of the law-governed international community. International law, like law in general, is predicated on equity and reason. Every principle of equity and every measure of right reason argue for the full participation of the ROC in the U.N. These, together with compelling pragmatic considerations, call for ROC membership in all regional and international bodies.

Upon arrival at the airport
in Singapore on January 2,
1994, Premier and Mrs. Lien
are warmly welcomed by
Singaporean Prime Minister
Goh Chok Tong and Mrs. Goh.

The Republic of China on Taiwan Belongs in the United Nations

An Article Appearing in the *Orbis* Quarterly,
United States
September 30, 1993

The world has undergone profound changes in the last few years. Some of the changes are having positive effects on mankind, such as the advent of new technology that allows us to communicate at will throughout the world, thus eroding boundaries between nations. The collapse of the USSR in 1991 removed the threat of nuclear war, thus making the globe a safer place and allowing the world to concentrate its attention on economic development instead of military and political confrontation. But the changes have also brought about new problems. Ethnic conflicts, long dormant, have re-emerged in some regions. Several countries, formerly torn asunder by political differences, are seeking readjustments of their borders, while others are initiating new conflicts. Europe and North America are making regional economic arrangements that may develop into exclusive economic blocs. Concerned by this prospect, nations of the Asia-Pacific region are also searching for ways to meet the new challenge. All in all, the changes are so revolutionary as to force nations to reconsider their priorities and interests in order to adjust to the new world order.

The Republic of China on Taiwan, having been on the leading edge of these changes with its political democratization and economic liberalization, has also developed a new set of priorities with a pragmatic approach.

Since 1949, the ROC on Taiwan has progressed from a war-ravaged, economically backward state to one of the most dynamic economies of the world, an accomplishment universally referred to as an "economic miracle." We are now the 14th largest trading nation in the world, and our per capita income has grown from US$70 to over US$10,000 today, ranking 25th in the world. We have the world's largest foreign exchange reserves. Although our growth rate has dropped recently from double to single digits, it is still impressive compared with the rest of the world. However, we have paid a price for our economic growth, particularly in the area of the environment. We are now taking actions to repair the damage in this respect.

While our economy boomed in the 1970s, the Republic of China suffered a series of diplomatic setbacks that would have relegated most nations to oblivion. In an effort to befriend the communist regime on the Chinese mainland, for geopolitical reasons, many powerful nations that had long supported the Republic of China switched their recognition from Taipei to Peking. As a result, the ROC was forced to withdraw from the United Nations in 1971; Japan recognized the mainland regime in 1972 and the United States followed suit in 1979. This development deprived the ROC of a large measure of its legal status in the international community, despite its continued possession of all the prerequisites of a sovereign state. We acknowledge the criticism that this diplomatic isolation was in a sense self-imposed because of our claim to represent the whole of China. But we have to point out that both we and the mainland regime, in the heat of our mutual hostility, participated in the creation of this situation. To this day, in fact, the mainland still refuses to have diplomatic relations with any country that recognizes the Republic of China on Taiwan. Many nations, enamored by the strategic importance of the mainland and the prospects of a huge market there, have played into the hands of the mainland regime by adhering to the concept in international law that discourages interference in the internal affairs of another nation. Consequently, the ROC on Taiwan, one of the most economically successful nations in the world and one which possesses all of the attributes of statehood, is not fully accepted as a member of the international community.

The Republic of China, responding to this problem and the recent changes worldwide, has now adopted a pragmatic stance in an effort to regain its rightful place in the world political and diplomatic arena.

Pragmatism in Foreign Relations

Under the leadership of President Lee Teng-hui, the ROC on Taiwan has embarked on a new approach to foreign relations that is quite different from the traditional approach to diplomacy and is perhaps not practiced by any other government today. Based on the fact that the Republic of China is an independent, sovereign nation on Taiwan, President Lee proposed pragmatic diplomacy to promote "our national development and position in the international community." We hope that by this approach we will eventually persuade the world to adjust to the reality that there are two political entities in China, separated by the Taiwan Straits. The sine qua non for pragmatic foreign relations is to accept a situation as it exists and a willingness to adjust to change. This approach takes into account the inflexible and unrealistic traditional diplomatic protocol that characterizes relations between nations.

In the spirit of pragmatism, we continue to do all in our power to enhance and enlarge the scope of our relations with the 29 countries with which we maintain formal diplomatic ties. As to nations that do not recognize us diplomatically, we have developed various forms of ties that allow near normal transactions to take place between us. We now have 89 representative offices in these countries, performing functions similar to embassies and consulates.

Public diplomacy is another aspect of our pragmatic foreign policy. We encourage and assist all segments of our society to participate in international activities, to help remind the world of the continuing existence of the Republic of China on Taiwan. Examples of this effort include the exhibition abroad of artifacts from our National Palace Museum, the participation of our Little League baseball teams in the World Championship in Williamsport, Pennsylvania, and the particpation of our ROC representative team in the Olympic Games.

But the current state of our foreign relations does not allow us to participate fully in all international activities. Even in the area of humanitarian relief, our assistance to refugees has had to go through various subterfuges, instead of the front door of international organizations. To rectify the situation, the Republic of

China must join international organizations and participate in their activities.

Re-entry into the United Nations

To achieve this goal, we have to make the world aware of our qualifications for membership in the international organizations, including the United Nations. President Lee has directed a major campaign to seek the ROC's re-entry into the United Nations. We believe that the ROC, as one of the original founders of the organization and a sovereign state that fulfilled all its obligations without reservation while a member of the organization until 1971, is entitled to participate in the world body. Although we do not seek to displace the mainland regime in the United Nations, we are aware of the possibility that the mainland will do all in its power to keep us out. We hope that the international community would reject the mainland's efforts against us, because there is no logical reason to deny the ROC the right to sit in the world body. Besides its economic strength, the ROC meets all the qualifications of U.N. membership. Moreover, the communist regime on the mainland has neither represented the ROC on Taiwan in the past, nor does it represent the 20 million people on Taiwan today. To continue excluding the ROC from the United Nations is both immoral and unrealistic. After all, both East Germany and West Germany were members of the United Nations before their unification, while the two Koreas also sit in the U.N. General Assembly simultaneously.

As the ROC takes stock of its position in the world, its leaders believe that the time is ripe to remind the world that the United Nations should be representative of all the nations of the world who are willing to adhere to its principles. The United Nations certainly should not be mired in traditional protocol that does not face reality. If the world body is to effectively accomplish its mission of maintaining world peace and promoting the welfare of mankind, it must observe its principle of universality. It is clear that such an attribute is not present in the exclusion of the ROC. We feel strongly that the United Nations should take up its moral responsibility by accepting all nations that are willing to join.

The "One China" Issue

The mainland regime has insisted on the "one China" principle as justification to deny the ROC's legal status in the international community. In our opinion, the mainland's position on "one China" is not only rigid and unreasonable, but contrary to Chinese history. It is true that ever since the unification of China by Chin Shih Huang Ti in 213 B.C., the Chinese people have believed in the concept of "one China." But they interpreted the concept in such a loose way that even in times of disunity, such as the Period of Three Kingdoms from 220 to 265 A.D., the Chinese people never thought that they deviated from this concept. In fact, the chronological chart of China's history shows that China has gone from a period of unity to one of separation and back again many times. The situation that exists today between Taiwan and the mainland merely represents another of the historical cycles.

The separate existence of two political entities does not mean that China will not be unified again at some future time. By the same account, the hope for an eventual

Chinese unification should not be used as a justification to deny the existence of two separate political entities with equal access to the international community. It is true that since 1949 both the ROC government and the mainland authorities claimed to be the legitimate ruler of whole China, including the territory occupied by the other. This, however, has changed in recent years. While the mainland continues to trumpet its claims over Taiwan, the ROC now accepts the reality that there are two political entities in China existing alongside each other. We interpret the current situation as "one China, two political entities." The mainland, on the other hand, takes the position of "one China, two systems," which pretends that the mainland has jurisdiction over the free people in the Taiwan area. This, the Republic of China cannot and will not accept.

Changes in Cross-Straits Relations

Three stages characterize relations between the ROC on Taiwan and mainland China since 1949. Military conflict marked the years from 1949 through 1978. In 1979, after the United States switched diplomatic recognition from Taipei to Peking, relations across the Taiwan Straits entered a period of peaceful confrontation. Then, in 1987, our former president Chiang Ching-kuo ordered a relaxation of rules to permit private-sector exchanges through third countries, specifically visits by ROC citizens to their relatives on the mainland. He took the step out of compassion for those people who had suffered long-term separation from their families on the mainland because of the conflict between the two sides. Visits to relatives quickly expanded to commercial and other contacts. As a result of the proliferating indirect contacts, more than 4.6 million persons from Taiwan have visited the mainland in the last five-and-a-half years, 64 million letters have been exchanged, and over 50 million telephone calls made between the two sides. By conservative estimates, indirect trade between Taiwan and the mainland has reached US$25.6 billion, while over ten thousand businessmen from Taiwan have invested a total of US$6.4 billion in the mainland.

Expansion of the indirect private-sector contacts naturally brought about a number of problems. One of the most persistent among them has been verification of documents. Without a mechanism to certify marriage, inheritance, academic records, and so forth, many people who engaged in cross-Straits activities have found themselves stuck in a legal black hole, unable to have their transactions legalized. Furthermore, while more than 64 million letters have been exchanged, there is no means to check, trace, or compensate for lost registered mail. Nor is there a legal framework to guarantee the protection of the millions of dollars of investments on the mainland by businessmen from Taiwan. Travellers from Taiwan are also at the mercy of unsafe carriers on the mainland. These are only a few of the many problems that have arisen from the expanding indirect exchange between the two sides of the Taiwan Straits. It is obvious that some kind of overarching framework is now required to deal with them.

A Blueprint for Reunification

An overall review of the situation across the Taiwan Straits makes clear the difficulties that have arisen from contacts between the two sides, as well as the need for the Republic of China to be properly accepted by the world community. With this understanding, the Republic of China on Taiwan now looks at the issue of Chinese reunification in a new pragmatic way. It is convinced that an immediate unification of China is impossible. The political and economic systems of the two sides of the Straits are so disparate that any hasty action toward unification would cause future discord. It is clear that more time is needed to allow the two sides to grow closer before a viable unification is possible.

After reevaluating the current situation, we designed a flexible blueprint for our relations with the mainland called *Guidelines for National Unification*. This blueprint calls for, first of all, the removal of obstacles between the two societies in order to facilitate mutually beneficial exchanges, and establish mutual trust to replace suspicion and hostility. If followed in good faith by the two sides, this plan will lead eventually to peaceful reunification of the two Chinese societies under a system of governance that will guarantee democracy, freedom, and an equal opportunity for all to pursue economic prosperity.

The goal of a united China that is democratic, free, and equitable is of utmost importance to the Republic of China in order to protect its way of life. Anything less would not be acceptable to the people of Taiwan. We believe the people on the mainland also aspire to the same goal, and hope that the mainland rulers will not reject the plan.

Under the aforementioned *Guidelines*, unification will be achieved in three stages. The first is a short-term stage of indirect contacts designed to remove mutual hostility, followed by a mid-term phase of mutual trust and cooperation when official contacts are allowed. The final, long-term stage will see the two sides holding consultations with each other to work out a program for reunification. We firmly believe that only through such a careful, stage-by-stage process can the individual interests of all Chinese be protected in the process of unification.

In the short-term stage, non-official intermediary bodies are established to resolve problems arising from private-sector contacts. These bodies are to meet with each other on a regular basis, not only to resolve practical problems but also to provide a momentum toward the establishment of mutual trust. Also essential to the build-up of this mutual trust, however, are the removal of the mainland's threat to invade Taiwan and its acceptance of the Republic of China as an equal political entity with the right to participate in international activities. Only when these conditions are met will the Republic of China on Taiwan be willing to enter the second phase of mutual trust and cooperation, the phase when official contacts are initiated. Direct postal relations, air and shipping services, and trade can also be established. There may also be economic cooperation between the two sides to help raise the standard of living on the mainland and, thus, remove one of the basic obstacles to unification.

Once hostility is replaced by mutual trust and cooperation, the people on both sides of the Straits will be in a position to move gradually into the third stage: actual unification. In this stage, a consultative body would be established to discuss the design of a future union aimed at bringing about a unified China that is democratic, free, and peace-loving, and guarantees social justice.

We are currently moving well into the first stage. The intermediary bodies of the two sides recently met in Singapore to discuss some of the practical problems that have arisen from the increasing private-sector contacts between the two sides. Although the mainland representative raised the issue of direct postal, transportation, and trade links in an attempt to move the cross-Straits relations prematurely into the second stage, representatives from the Republic of China successfully deflected this attempt and focused attention on the resolution of practical problems. Four agreements were signed at the end of the Singapore talks to establish procedures for the resolution of problems relating to document verification and registered mail. Agreement was also reached on regular meetings between the two unofficial bodies.

It may be noted that the Singapore talks were conducted on such an equal basis as to reinforce the Republic of China's right to participate in international affairs as a separate political entity.

Military Posture Across the Straits

A review of the situation in the Taiwan Straits must not overlook recent efforts by the mainland to beef up its military. Its large purchases of sophisticated weapon systems from the Commonwealth of Independent States, its continued sales of weapons of mass destruction to nations hostile to democracies, and its plan to build a blue-water navy, all have caused worry among Asian countries that the mainland might be adopting an expansionist policy in an attempt to fill the power vacuum left by the reduction of U.S. forces in the area. Such a policy would definitely endanger the peace and security of this region. Furthermore, the mainland still refuses to renounce the use of force on Taiwan, forcing the Republic of China to modernize its armed forces in order to maintain a military capability sufficient to defend itself. For this reason, the ROC must be allowed to purchase weapons from abroad.

It is not the Republic of China's policy to obtain an offensive capability for its armed forces. Our Ministry of National Defense is undertaking a restructuring program to streamline the armed forces, emphasizing quality rather than quantity, and making the necessary adjustments in force configuration. At the same time, we continue to develop our own defense industry so as to reduce reliance on foreign suppliers.

We hope we will never find it necessary to send our armed forces to battle. But we will not hesitate to defend ourselves when our security is threatened.

Regional Security and Economic Cooperation

Realizing a general concern in Asia about regional security, President Lee Teng-hui, as early as 1991, pointed to the need for a regional arrangement to discuss and arbitrate disputes before they deteriorate into uncontrollable economic and military conflicts. Lately, following the withdrawal of U.S. forces from the Philippines, the issue of a regional security arrangement has received widespread attention in Asia as well as the United States. U.S. allies and friends in this region have become increasingly concerned about their security, particularly their capability to cope with future threats from within the region. This Asian concern was further exacerbated by Japan's decision to send troops abroad and Chinese communist expansion of its naval force.

Perhaps the "new world order" idea expounded by former U.S. president George Bush can be applied to Asia to engender a new security framework for the Asia-Pacific region in which all states would participate. Such a multilateral, comprehensive security arrangement would serve the purposes of preserving regional stability and security and discouraging military build-up. Asian countries need a peaceful environment, so as to concentrate on economic development. A broad security framework will help provide such an environment.

The ROC has lent its strong support to such an Asia-Pacific security arrangement. On september 4, 1992, in a meeting with a group of distinguished Americans who were visiting the area to collect information for a report on U.S.-Asia policy in the post-Cold War era, President Lee discussed the possibility of creating such a new arrangement, telling them that the ROC is in a position to play an important part in the security system by virtue of its strategic location in the Western Pacific and its economic prosperity and political stability. During an interview with the Cable News Network on March 16, 1993, President Lee again expressed his hope that countries of the Asia-Pacific region would seriously consider such a security system, one which, with no specific enemy in mind, would resolve regional disputes through regular dialogue. The ROC stands ready to make its contribution to this system.

Looking to the Future

The Republic of China on Taiwan is acutely aware of the tremendous changes taking place in the world. We too are a part of these changes, and we are determined to participate as a full equal in the march toward a new world order. We have reevaluated our policies in realistic terms and developed pragmatic actions, policies, and programs that we feel will make our membership in the international community viable. We are not blind to the difficulties that lie ahead, but we believe that we have devised strategies that can help remove the obstacles. Working toward a peaceful unification of China is a positive step. But that step depends upon the full cooperation of the two political entities on either side of the Taiwan Straits. We realize that this task cannot be accomplished overnight, but we have the staying power to see it through to the end.

This article was originally printed in the Fall 1993 issue of *Orbis*.

Premier Lien (left) is invited to a dinner party by Singaporean President Ong Teng Cheong and the first lady on January 3, 1994.

Let the Cry for Justice Reach Far and Wide

Remarks on the 30th Anniversary of the National Press Council
September 2, 1993

Few people realize that over two years ago President Lee Teng-hui ordered the relevant government ministries to look into the issue of the ROC's participation in the United Nations, and had indicated that the ROC should begin to solicit understanding and support in the international community. Over the last two years, not only have the government and the opposition parties reached a measure of consensus over the issue, it has also been extensively covered by the media in Taiwan and abroad.

I can report to you that many voices favoring the ROC's participation in the United Nations have made themselves heard in the international media. For instance, newspapers in Boston, San Francisco, and other cities have recently carried letters to the editor submitted by the ROC government's information offices stationed abroad, calling to the attention of the American public the right of the ROC to participate in the United Nations. On July 3, 1993, the British Broadcasting Corporation broadcast a special program about the ROC's position on this issue. Likewise on August 4, 1993, *The West Australian* published an article written by David Goodman, head of the Asia Research Centre at Murdock University. In the article, Dr. Goodman, a scholar spe-

153

cializing in Chinese affairs, emphasized that if the United Nations excludes the ROC from participating, "the refusal of admittance...may limit the U.N.'s room for maneuver." The media in other countries, including Germany, Holland, France, and Belgium, have all conducted similar coverage that has directed international attention to the ROC's aspiration to expand the scope of its international activities and to participate in international organizations. Even more heartening, on August 6, 1993, seven Central American countries jointly forwarded a letter to U.N. Secretary-General Boutros Boutros-Ghali asking the United Nations to seriously consider the importance of parallel representation in the U.N. for the divided China and requesting the United Nations to find a feasible resolution of this issue.

The ROC Should Never Be Overlooked

Each time when I met with foreign dignitaries, I have explained with utmost clarity and sincerity why the ROC has adequate and sufficient cause to participate in the United Nations.

Since its withdrawal from the United Nations, the ROC has not disappeared from the world map. Instead, it has, thanks to the combined efforts of its people, won worldwide recognition for its extraordinary successes. Today, everyone knows that the ROC is the 14th largest trading nation in the world and holds foreign exchange reserves that rank either first or second in the world. The ROC has the world's 25th highest per capita income. In terms of population, the Republic of China on Taiwan is larger than two-thirds of the 184 member countries of the United Nations. By any standard, the ROC is a powerful country, entitled to a seat in the U.N.

Some people who supported the Chinese communists' entry into the United Nations emphasized that the world must not overlook the strength of the Chinese communists and that to isolate the Chinese communists would be disadvantageous to global interests. I think the same can now be said of the Republic of China. On November 10, 1990, the *New York Times* published an editorial, "Taiwan: Too Big to Ignore," which appealed to the United States and other nations to consider the existence and development of the Republic of China on Taiwan. This undoubtedly demonstrates that it would be unwise and inappropriate for the United Nations to continue to ignore the ROC. Many specialists in international affairs might have noticed that the United Nations and its peripheral organizations have rarely included in their publications the statistical information about the Republic of China on Taiwan. This omission has not only detracted from the thoroughness and usefulness of these publications, but has also encroached on the rights and interests of their users. This situation must be rectified quickly.

In addition, for the last few decades, Western democracies have stressed the importance of freedom and democracy. Today, the Republic of China on Taiwan has attained outstanding results in democratic reform. Several surveys have revealed that participation in the U.N. is the freely expressed desire of the majority of the people in the ROC. It would be inexcusable for any country that truly treasures freedom and respects democracy to pretend to not notice our aspirations.

Willing and Able to Make Contributions

It is particularly worth pointing out that the international community would certainly benefit practically from the ROC's participation in the United Nations. The ROC has both the will and the wherewithal to actively contribute to maintaining international order, to promoting economic and trade cooperation, and to providing international humanitarian relief. Everyone knows that the ROC has turned from an aid-receiver to an aid-giver in the last ten years. We began parceling out money from the International Disaster Relief Aid Fund in 1980. We established the International Economic Cooperation and Development Fund in 1988, and we have sent 43 technical cooperation teams to assist in the development of 31 countries. These actions demonstrate that the ROC has taken concrete steps to pay back the international community for its help in the past and is now serving as a contributor, partner, and participant to countries and regions in all stages of development.

The ROC is, regrettably, not a member of the United Nations and is often handicapped from carrying out its charitable missions to pay back the international community for what it has got from it. For instance, during the Gulf War two years ago, the ROC was poised to provide economic aid to some of the countries ravaged by the war. Who could have guessed that these countries had hesitations in accepting the aid just because the ROC is not a member of the United Nations? As a result, many delays and complications undermined the effectiveness of the aid. Another example was the recent global effort to ameliorate the worsening greenhouse effect. The United Nations launched a massive effort to protect the ozone layer and rallied various countries to sign the *Montreal Protocol*. Although the ROC wished to participate, it was excluded from the treaty strictly because the ROC is not a member country of the United Nations. This is not only unfair to a country that has the desire to participate in international cooperative efforts, but it also undermines the effective solution of environmental problems. Furthermore, it sets a bad precedent for political interference in environmental protection and inevitably "limit[s] the U.N.'s room for maneuver." Surely the United Nations must understand that without active global cooperation, the ability of mankind to resolve its common problems will be undermined. It is not unreasonable to expect the United Nations, as the highest international governing organ in the world, to abide by the principle of universality of membership.

Righting Wrongs and Restoring Justice

The ROC has yet another reason to assert its right to participate in the United Nations: The ROC wants to fight for the basic rights and dignity of the 21 million Chinese people in the Taiwan area. From the viewpoint of international law, the United Nations' *Universal Declaration of Human Rights* in 1948, *The International Covenant on Civil and Political Rights* in 1966, and *The International Covenant on Economic, Social and Cultural Rights* passed in the same year all emphasize that every person is entitled to participate in political, cultural, and economic activities. These are the fundamental rights and basic dignity of every person in the world, and these rights differ from the general rights that every government should guarantee. The people of the Republic of China have already enjoyed the full spectrum of general rights and we do not need others to help us in this respect. However, in the 22 years since we were excluded from the United Nations, the 21 million citizens in the Taiwan area have been seriously discriminated against and their dignity and basic rights to participate in political, economic, and cultural activities in the international community have been violated. This is a very immoral, unfair, and unreasonable situation. If the United Nations really values human rights, it must not continue to just sit by and watch. The United Nations should prove its esteem for human rights by promptly taking action to correct the situation and by compensating the 21 million people in the Taiwan area, whose rights have been violated. I firmly believe that the time has come for the international community, and in particular the United Nations, to rectify the situation and to restore justice.

Members of the United Nations must realize that while the U.N. Assembly, in its 1971 resolution, accepted the Chinese communist authorities and barred us from its organizations, the U.N., nevertheless, ignored the fact that the Chinese communists cannot and are not entitled to represent the 21 million people in the Republic of China on Taiwan. We are not represented in the United Nations today. Nor do we have anyone who can stand up for our rights or promise to take on our responsibilities. Is it normal for such an important international intergovernmental organization to ignore the existence of our 21 million people? Is it normal for our children, women, aged, and handicapped to be excluded from U.N. activities and deprived of their rights and the benefits which their counterparts in other countries around the world enjoy? Is it normal for our police to be deprived of full international cooperation in their mission to crack down on international crimes and drug trafficking?

Joining the U.N. Helps National Unification

Of course, we all realize that the greatest resistance to our participation in the U.N. comes from the Chinese communists. I strongly disapprove of the various actions taken by the Chinese communists in the last few days to suppress us in the international community in an attempt to thwart our participation in the United Nations. The Chinese communists should face reality. If they cannot rationally and practically think through this issue and examine this very serious question, they will betray their solemn obligation to the Chinese people.

The ROC is entitled to enjoy its rightful national status, even prior to unification. The ROC's decision to participate in the U.N. is not intended to create a permanent split between the two sides of the Taiwan Straits. On the contrary, the ROC believes that participation in the U.N. would increase our confidence in the unification of China and trigger more active measures to pursue the eventual unification of China according to the *Guidelines for National Unification*. The Chinese communists would be enlightened if they would only look at the classic case of East Germany and West Germany, which were simultaneous members of the United Nations and yet unified without any obstacles. North Korea and South Korea serve as another example of simultaneous participation by a divided nation in the United

Nations and the best evidence that the two political entities can simultaneously belong to an international organization. Whether in terms of theory or in terms of practice, the ROC's advocacy of participation in the United Nations is reasonable and feasible. The ROC's position on this issue is totally clear. The ROC's efforts to participate in the United Nations must be carried out in line with the principle of a unified China, and will certainly have positive effects on the eventual unification of China. We hope that the Chinese communist authorities will calmly evaluate the situation and not impede the unification of China.

The Chinese communists must realize that the United Nations was formed in the aftermath of the Second World War when mankind had set its will on pursuing peace after having experienced bloodshed and catastrophe. Therefore, the highest ideal of the United Nations is to turn swords into plowshares, or as the Chinese would say, turn hostility into friendship. A renowned Western scholar of international relations, David Mitrany, once placed emphasis on "peace by pieces." The Republic of China has always been a peace-loving nation and its intention to rejoin the United Nations is based on its sincere desire to promote peace in the world and in China. The Chinese communists should not oppose the numerous opportunities for bi-coastal contact and interaction provided by international forums. Is it possible that the Chinese communists are opposed to fostering bi-coastal understanding and mutual trust through such contacts and interaction? Can they be opposed to working for "peace by pieces" to pave the way for the peaceful unification of the Chinese people?

Time to Work for U.N. Membership

Of course, it should be emphasized that we know we are entitled to participate in the United Nations, that we are strengthened by this knowledge, and that we realize that we must do our best. We shall not weaken in the face of opposition from either the Chinese communists or anyone else. We are confident that our future status in the international community will be commensurate with the expansion of our national strength. The scope for our international activities can only continue to expand, regardless of any plans to obstruct us. If we are only willing to work hard, we will surely gain strength, and if we are strong, we will surely have a future — a future that will not depend on the Chinese communists or on any outsider. The ROC will determine its own future.

Ladies and gentlemen, President Lee once reminded us that "to be alive is to have hope." Today, the ROC is not merely alive, it has taken a forceful first step in its bid to participate in the United Nations. We know, however, that a long and winding path lies before us. Nevertheless, participation in the United Nations is not an unattainable dream. If we only bolster our confidence, redouble our efforts, unite all the people, consolidate national resources, and if the government and the opposition parties are of one mind, then the ROC can cast an even greater influence on the international community. In this way, I believe the ROC can gain international support and attain its goal of participating in the United Nations.

Let the Cry for Justice Reach Far

I sincerely hope that the National Press Council will expand its pervasive influence on the mass media, and through various media and communication channels, spread our calls and our expectations to every corner of the globe. Let the cry for justice spread far and wide. Let us create more opportunities to participate in the activities of the United Nations, so that we can finally participate in that organization at an early date.

III. Mainland Initiatives

A joyful reunion with an
old friend on January 4, 1991
— Premier Lien (right) and
former Singaporean Prime
Minister Lee Kuan Yew.

Nurturing Mutual Trust and Moving toward Mutual Gain

Opening Remarks to the 1994 Mainland Work Conference
July 4, 1994

Our mainland work is a complex and important business full of challenges. It directly affects the survival and development of our nation and has far-reaching impact on the prosperity and future of the Chinese people. In the past, mainland affairs were handled separately by the various ministries and agencies under whose purview they fell. But in January 1991, power and responsibility were centralized by the Executive Yuan which set up the Mainland Affairs Council to plan, coordinate and promote mainland affairs. The purpose for this momentous decision was to meet the needs of the times and circumstances in hopes of combining the forces of all ministries and agencies to promote mainland affairs in a planned, procedural, comprehensively thought-out and careful manner and thereby give impetus to the positive growth of cross-Straits relations.

Looking back to November 2, 1987, the ROC government broke the ice of 40 years and formally liberalized its citizens' visits to relatives on the mainland. This opened a new chapter in person-to-person cross-Straits exchange and created a new relationship of cross-Straits interaction. Over the past six years or so, for the future of the nation and in order to further cross-Straits relations, we have demonstrated goodwill to the greatest extent possible in accordance with our pre-set policy and position. Private-sector exchanges have become quite frequent: Every year there are more than one million visits back and forth. Indirect trade exceeds US$10 billion, and postal and telephone traffic is becoming increasingly intensive. Through such intensive cross-Straits exchanges at the personal level, both sides have amassed a great deal of valuable experience and have increased mutual familiarity and understanding, thereby laying an important foundation for moving toward national reunification.

Even though we have demonstrated the greatest sincerity and goodwill in advancing cross-Straits relations and have taken concrete steps, the reunification strategy of the Chinese communist authorities has remained set in stone. They are unwilling to face the present reality that the Republic of China exists and is vigorous. Accordingly, it is still impossible to establish an order for cross-Straits interaction and exchange, nor is it yet possible to bring about the communication of concepts. These difficulties and obstacles have caused cross-Straits relations to remain in an unstable state of peaceful stalemate. The foundation of mutual trust between the two sides is still very weak. At the end of March this year, the occurrence of the Qiandao Lake Incident in Zhejiang Province further exacerbated this unstable condition as a result of bungling by the Chinese communist Zhejiang authorities, underscoring the severity of these difficulties and obstacles.

The ROC government has consistently sought national reunification, not for a single day abandoning this goal since 1949. We must continue striving to realize this objective. In February 1991, the National Unification Council of the Office of the President laid down the *Guidelines for National Unification*, which were endorsed by the Executive Yuan Council the following month. It is explicitly declared in the *Guidelines* that we have as our goal the pursuit of a democratic, free, equitably prosperous and unified China. This document constitutes the clearest expression of the ROC government's national reunification policy.

In order to pursue the objective proclaimed by the *Guidelines for National Unification*, the ROC government has advocated the principles of reason, peace, parity and reciprocity as prerequisites for positive interaction in promoting cross-Straits relations. In terms of concrete practice, we have taken the initiative and announced the termination of the Period of National Mobilization for Suppression of the Communist Rebellion, nullified the *Temporary Provisions* effective during that period, and through legal procedures have expressed our determination to adopt peaceful methods to achieve national reunification. We have also pragmatically acknowledged the present situation of division between Taiwan and the mainland and their separate political rule. In terms of cross-Straits relations, we have proposed the advocacy of "one nation, two areas," and "two equal political entities," thereby avoiding disputes about internal political relationships or diplomatic relations and enabling us to move toward national unification at full blast.

The ROC government has repeatedly declared that it does not advocate "Taiwan independence," nor does it accede to "one China, one Taiwan," "two Chinas," or other similar ideas. At the same time, however, we absolutely refuse to accept deliberate misinterpretations of our actions to promote cross-Straits relations, or any doubts or criticisms concerning our government's sincerity and determination.

As the development of cross-Straits relations depends on mutual interaction, mutual trust is an essential factor here. The crux of our entering into the medium phase outlined in the *Guidelines for National Unification* lies in the establishment of mutual trust between Taiwan and the mainland. President Lee clearly pointed out in his 1994 New Year's Day address that this is the year for nurturing mutual trust between the two sides. Last year, I proposed the ideal of renouncing "zero sum" and proceeding towards "win-win." Mutual trust and "win-win" are two sides of a coin. Without mutual trust, we will ultimately remain stuck in the "zero sum" rut, unable to create new openings for national reunification.

National reunification is a formidable project. The great differences between the systems and concepts on the two sides have already prolonged the journey to reunification. For the future of the nation and the people, Taiwan and mainland China share the responsibility to participate in this project. Both are also obliged to bridge the gaps between the two sides so that they can proceed with exchanges and interactions in a more open, free and pluralistic manner.

I would like to raise a few points on how to foster mutual trust and realize our "win-win" policy.

First of all, no damage to cross-Straits relations should be done. The quest on both sides of the Straits for national reunification is not confined to so narrow a goal as territorial reunification or a formalistic reunification of political rule but consists rather of working for the welfare of all Chinese people and for the long-term development of the Chinese nation. Therefore, the quest for reunification is in no way a life-or-death struggle in which each is at the other's throat, but rather a common goal to be realized through the exercise of supreme wisdom. The exercise of any coercive or threatening conduct toward each other can in no way help realize the goal of reunification but will merely work to the detriment of cross-Straits relations and impair the progress of reunification.

Secondly, we should try to understand each other's position and trust each other's behavior. The political systems on the two sides of the Straits differ considerably. A modern democratic system is being gradually completed in the Taiwan area while the progress of political reforms in the mainland area is still quite limited. Under this premise, the administrative actions of the Republic of China government must be based on the will of the people, while on the mainland there is still a tendency toward centralized rule. This is what both sides should acknowledge. In other words, under the norms of democracy and the rule of law, the policies of the Republic of China government have demonstrated stability, endurance and consistency. The Chinese communist authorities should observe and understand our national reunification policy and determination from this point of view. Only then can the gap of mutual trust be narrowed.

Thirdly, the cross-Straits relationship should produce goodwill. I deeply believe that goodwill is an important factor in fostering mutual trust. Over the past three years, the Republic of China government has declared the termination of the Period of National Mobilization for Suppression of the Communist Rebellion, and initiated many measures of extreme goodwill for the cross-Straits relationship. Given that the Chinese communists are still profoundly antagonistic toward us, the significance of these measures for productive interaction between the two sides is all the more evident. While antagonism remains unabated, there is no basis for mutual trust. A gradual diminution of antagonism represents the steady growth of mutual trust. We hope that the Chinese communist authorities can keenly perceive this and create the necessary goodwill for cross-Straits relations as soon as possible.

Fourthly, national sentiment should be correctly interpreted and expressed. National sentiment has been repeatedly emphasized over thousands of years of Chinese history. While such sentiment is the original impetus for both sides of the Straits to work towards national reunification, any misrepresentation or manipulation of this sentiment can only wound genuine national sentiment to the point where no one is willing to advocate it further. The Republic of China government has, since its establishment in 1912, followed the teachings left by Dr. Sun Yat-sen, and fully incorporated the Principle of Nationalism in government administration. Therefore, the ultimate goal of our national reunification policy is to work for the greatest welfare of the Chinese people as a whole. To merely pay lip service to the Principle of Nationalism while overlooking the welfare of the people would be a distortion of national sentiment, while using military force toward the other side would be even more at odds with national sentiment.

172

Over the past several years, the staff members of pertinent government agencies have devoted a great deal of effort and wisdom to promoting the positive development of cross-Straits relations. Looking to the future, we will face many more and many greater problems and challenges. Therefore, how to combine our forces and make the appropriate plans and preparations in advance should be the common goal of all staff members. It is my hope that all of us will continue making efforts in the following areas:

■ Our mainland affairs policies are characteristically decided collectively. Therefore, we should step up mutual coordination and communication prior to arriving at a policy. Once a policy is established, it should be implemented completely with full cooperation and in concert.

■ Every ministry and agency should gradually bolster its ability to handle mainland affairs. The success or failure of mainland affairs policies is not just the responsibility of the Mainland Affairs Council but also that of each ministry and agency concerned. As cross-Straits relations develop, the quality and quantity of mainland affairs to be dealt with will certainly increase. Every ministry and agency concerned must take appropriate measures to gradually strengthen its ability to deal with them. It is also hoped that the MAC, based on its professional position, will then help the staff members of each ministry or agency concerned enrich their knowledge and capabilities.

■ There ought to be appropriate norms for issuing public statements about mainland affairs. Mainland affairs often involve sensitive issues. Especially when cross-Straits relations are still rocky and both sides lack mutual trust, should a staff member of any agency concerned make public an unnecessary or not yet fully coordinated opinion, it might confuse the public or even create a misunderstanding or exacerbate hostility between the two sides of the Straits. Consequently, any rhetoric about mainland affairs by a ministry or agency should be made prudently and responsibly after reaching consensus.

National reunification is one of the most important goals of future governmental administration. We have consistently shown the greatest sincerity in promoting the positive development of cross-Straits relations. I want to once again call upon the Chinese communists to immediately summon their highest wisdom and greatest courage and face the reality that the two sides of the Straits are separate and ruled by two different entities, out of consideration for the future of the country and for the development of the Chinese nation. They should promote cross-Straits relations with sincerity and good faith, disavow at the earliest date the tactic of disparaging our status, renounce the hostility which runs counter to nationalism, realize the priority and importance of mutual trust and reciprocity, and sincerely accept our "win-win" proposal.

The theme of this conference is to "Realize Exchange and Reciprocity; Promote Positive Interaction." Fully carrying out this theme really depends on all participants in the meeting evaluating the past with open minds, and working out future plans pragmatically. By contributing our wisdom and experience, we can charter the most appropriate course for our future mainland policy, and propose the best solution to further cross-Straits relations.

In a formal visit to Guatemala
in June 1994, Premier Lien dis-
cusses strengthening bilateral
relations with President Ramiro
de León Carpio.

From "Zero Sum" to "Win-Win": Changing the Basis of the Cross-Straits Relationship

An Address to the Executive Yuan Press Association
December 17, 1993

The extent to which a country allows freedom of the press and the free exchange of information indicates just how politically developed and modernized that country really is. The media are the guides and critics of the government. Your guidance and encouragement spur the Executive Yuan to seek constant improvement. Joining the ranks of the media is the most direct way for an intellectual to serve his community and his nation.

After taking office, I have become more convinced than ever before that, in light of the Republic of China's current international status, we must use our wisdom to find a better solution to questions regarding our relationship with the Chinese mainland. For a long time, Taiwan and the Chinese mainland had no contact or exchange except in the form of military confrontation and political and diplomatic contention. Our impressions of each other basically were based on Cold War antagonisms. These rigid stereotypes led to further misunderstanding and even outright conflict. Such a situation was a losing proposition for both sides. To break through the impasse, the ROC government on November 2, 1987 took the initiative and allowed residents of Taiwan to visit their relatives in the Chinese mainland. This decision has had a profound impact on cross-Straits relations.

177

Under the direction of President Lee, a National Unification Council was set up within the Office of the President in 1990, and the *Guidelines for National Unification* were adopted the following year. The *Guidelines* call for unifying China in phases in accordance with the principles of reason, peace, parity, and reciprocity. Moreover, an organizational framework was created through the revision and amendment of the ROC Constitution and through the passage of the *Statute Governing Relations Between People of the Taiwan Area and the Mainland Area*. By codifying our approach to relations with the Chinese mainland, we have vastly strengthened our policy-making process. The Koo-Wang Talks held in Singapore this April further institutionalized channels of communication between the two sides of the Taiwan Straits and initiated a series of talks between our Straits Exchange Foundation and the Chinese mainland's Association for Relations Across the Taiwan Straits.

It is, nonetheless, difficult to be satisfied with developments in cross-Straits relations. Perhaps, our difficulties are due to prejudices stemming from our forty years of separation. The ideological, political, social, and economic systems championed by the two sides are still too far apart. In particular, many moves taken by the mainland authorities in recent months, including their release of a white paper titled *The Taiwan Question and Reunification of china*, their blocking of ROC participation in the United Nations, and their high-handed talk on sovereignty during the Asia-Pacific Economic Cooperation summit in Seattle have shown that the animosity of the past still prevails in relations between the two sides of the Taiwan Straits.

Mutual credibility, it seems, is still an elusive goal. To promote positive interaction between the two sides of the Taiwan Straits and accelerate our entry into the medium phase outlined in the *Guidelines for National Unification*, the two sides must patiently work to establish mutual understanding and trust.

On November 2, while responding to the interpellations of legislators, I stated that if the Chinese communist authorities could take account of the international situation and consider the current changes in and future prospects for cross-Straits relations, the two sides of the Straits could then embark on the path to a "win-win" conclusion. In other words, if the Chinese communists really want to pursue the unification of China and foster positive development between the two sides of the Straits, they must try to understand our ideas and positions by adopting a pragmatic and rational attitude and facing up to the fact that there are two distinct political entities on the two sides of the Straits. If the Chinese communists, however, continue to insist on the "one country, two systems" model, regard us as a local government, refuse to give up the use of force against Taiwan, and ignore the desire of the people in Taiwan to play a more active international role, then there can be no hope of expunging the antagonism between us and establishing a mutually beneficial and reciprocal relationship marked by trust and cooperation.

The Chinese communists have not responded positively to the *Guidelines for National Unification*, which are based on the "one China" principle. Rather, they have mobilized their media and academic sectors to distort and to criticize the *Guidelines*. The full text of the *Guide-*

lines has never been published or openly discussed in the Chinese mainland. This not only violates the right of the people in the mainland to know what is going on, it also deprives them of any way to learn about our unification policy. The people in the Chinese mainland are left with no real choices, and we are left to wonder whether the Chinese communist authorities really want national unification. Blocking the free flow of information is a misguided move that, in the end, hinders the peaceful unification of China.

An environment for peaceful interaction between the two sides of the Taiwan Straits is already taking shape. Based on the spirit of regional cooperation in the Asia-Pacific region, each side of the Straits can make up for the other's economic shortcomings. As for participating in international organizations, the United Nations is an ideal forum for communication. No one can deny that two political entities do exist on the two sides of the Taiwan Straits. Why should we indulge in a destructive competition by rejecting such a reality? Why should we continue to waste so many developmental resources that could benefit the people? Could it be that the Chinese mainland authorities are really unable to come up with a forward-looking plan, to seek cross-Straits cooperation from a historic perspective, and to create a brighter future for the Chinese people? Do they really want to take a path that will lead to our mutual destruction rather than opting for a "win-win" solution?

Man's thirst for information is innate. The development of modern broadcasting technology is such that political intervention can only momentarily block the flow of information. Cross-Straits interaction would naturally move in a positive direction if the Chinese communist authorities would only listen to reason, respect the people's right to know, and promote the flow of information between the two sides of the Straits. The information exchanges need not be a tool for "exporting revolution," "carrying out united front tactics," or "peaceful evolution." The exchange of information is the only path to mutual trust and cooperation, peace and security, and prosperous development. In face of the global trend of democratization, political leaders should carefully bear in mind that a closed-door policy is against the tide of the times and is surely doomed to fail.

Today, therefore, I would like to most sincerely call upon the Chinese communist authorities to accept our goodwill and sincerity, and join with us to bring about information exchanges in the following four areas:

■ Media and Communications — The two sides of the Taiwan Straits should abandon politically-oriented media confrontation. Rather, the Chinese communists should, in accordance with the principle of parity, lift their restrictions on the exchange of news, motion pictures, television programs, videotapes, and printed materials. The two sides should hold talks on the mutual protection of copyrights. We should hold film festivals, book fairs and other similar kinds of events on both sides of the Straits. Newspapers from both sides should be encouraged to set up cooperative relationships and to establish channels for the flow of information. Each side should permit the import of newspapers from the other side and should relax restrictions on stationing reporters or establishing branch offices on each other's territory. We should allow the private sector to promote mutual

181

understanding and reduce ideological differences through the unimpeded exchange of information.

■ Economy and Finance — The two sides should exchange information on business management, trade, and financing. We should implement a policy of encouraging the accumulation of wealth in the private sector and implement a more open market economy that would allow for more efficient distribution of resources between the two sides of the Taiwan Straits. This, in turn, would enable us to agree on a mutually beneficial division of productive labor. The mainland would serve as China's industrial heartland, and Taiwan would serve as the operations center of the Asia-Pacific region. By capitalizing on the economic advantages of the two areas, we could bring about a rapid rise in the gross national product and continued improvement in the living standards of the people. Slowly but surely, the economic disparity between the two sides would even out.

■ Culture and Art — Cultural and artistic exchanges should be allowed. The two sides ought to lift restrictions on top performing troupes and artists who would like to study and perform on both sides of the Taiwan Straits. Information on culture and arts should be collected and exchanged. We could selectively revive certain artistic traditions that are now in danger of dying out. The two sides should also calmly discuss standardizing written Chinese. Starting with the unification of written characters, we should gradually reduce differences in our understanding of culture. Representatives from the arts communities in Taiwan and the Chinese mainland should hold symposiums on arts and culture, and, via the free exchange of opinions, reduce the cultural differences between the two sides of the Taiwan Straits.

■ Science and Technology — The two sides should put the native intelligence of the Chinese people to work by exchanging information on cutting-edge science and technology. Scientists and researchers should be allowed to travel freely between the two sides of the Taiwan Straits. In particular, we should exchange scientific and technological information on natural disaster prevention and relief, and on agricultural and fishery production technology. Such exchanges would raise production quality, cut down on pollution, and reduce the technological gap between Taiwan and the Chinese mainland.

We in the Taiwan area place a high value on the free exchange of information, and we have high expectations for the mainland authorities when it comes to information exchanges. The unimpeded flow of information played an important and constructive role in the reunification of Germany. The two sides of the Taiwan Straits can learn from this experience. We would especially like to call upon the Chinese communist authorities to understand our good intentions and our conviction, and to respect our sincerity and patience. They should leave behind the "It's either you or me" zero-sum conflict and join us to create a "win-win" situation.

We should always remember that the people in Taiwan and the mainland are members of the same family. A "win-win" policy is the best guarantee for restoring the grandeur of the Chinese people. Information exchanges are essential to our common destiny. By learning from each other and complementing each other's strengths and weaknesses, we can shorten the road to national unification. We don't want the Taiwan experience to be our pride alone, but hope to make it an asset of all Chinese people to savor together. Armed with reason, optimism, and vision, let us close the gulf that divides us through the exchange of information. For in so doing, we can naturally achieve the unification of China and go on to create a brilliant new era for the Chinese people in the coming century.

IV. Interviews

The premier listens attentively to a briefing during his
inspection of a military in-
stallation on Kinmen on June
21, 1993.

The Premier's Plans and Goals for the Future

Responses to Written Questions Submitted by *World Statesman* Magazine, United Kingdom
August 1993

Taiwan's economic growth in the past decades has been spectacular. How do you gauge the current strength of the economy?

The high economic growth rates in the ROC over the past few decades, a joint achievement of the government and people, have been apparent to all. In the past few years, however, the ROC economy has maintained a moderate growth rate of 6 percent to 7 percent as it has moved towards greater maturity and been influenced by fluctuations in the international economy. In view of the general doldrums of the world economy in the last year or two, a moderate growth was a spectacular achievement. Although we are faced with sluggish investment, a less than ideal quality of life, and an outflow of capital, our Six-Year National Development Plan has set in motion our public construction, scientific R&D, and the cultivation of a talented work force. Our performance in these fields has won international recognition. Now we have launched an Economic Stimulus Package and are pushing it at full tilt aimed at redressing the foregoing problems in order to create a "second spring" for our economic development. To succeed, we count on our forty years of experience in economic development and our abundant human resources, which are the foundation of our economic strength.

Despite a weak international economic recovery, the ROC still has the strength to score a 6.33 percent economic growth rate in 1993. In an investigative report released by the U.S. Conference Board in March 1992, the ROC was ranked first in terms of economic performance and economic circulation index among 11 industrial countries including the United States, Canada, Germany, France, the United Kingdom, Italy, Japan, and South Korea. The English magazine *Euromoney* also predicted in September 1992 that the ROC would rank first in overall economic performance among all these countries. We will not let these reports go to our head. We will keep striving to overcome the difficulties confronting us and to break through our economic bottlenecks. In this way, we can sustain our economic growth as we are marching towards the goal of becoming a developed country.

Planning, as much as the free market, helped to turn Taiwan into one of Asia's economic "dragons" along with South Korea, Singapore and Hong Kong; but will there be as much emphasis on economic planning in the future?

In light of the world trend towards economic liberalization, the ROC government should avoid excessive interference. However, due to the limited supply of natural resources in the Taiwan area and the enormous complexity of its development tasks, the formulation of economic development plans cannot be overlooked. We will continue to uphold the basic principles of the market economy and let the private sector play the dominant role in economic development. The government will provide incentives by mapping out future national economic development plans in accordance with both the domestic and the international situations and the requirements of the particular phase of development, which set forth appropriate economic targets and development priorities. We hope this will lead to effective use of resources and speed up the economic development.

Trade with the Chinese communists have increased in recent years, reaching around US$6 billion in 1992. Is this a deliberate policy initiative on the part of your government, and in what way does the economic relationship with the Chinese communists differ from that with your other trading partners?

The Chinese mainland has accelerated its reform and opening-up in recent years. Most countries have increased their trade with the mainland area. Investment by Taiwanese businessmen there has also grown quickly, and the subsequent bi-coastal trade has expanded accordingly. According to Chinese communists' statistics, the amount of capital that Taiwanese businessmen have agreed to invest in the mainland had reached US$8.99 billion by the end of 1992. Moreover, according to statistics by Hong Kong Customs, the bi-coastal transshipment trade reached as high as US$7.41 billion in 1992. These were results of business behavior motivated by profit — a natural trend beyond our government's influence.

For many years, the ROC has aimed consistently at liberalization and internationalization in its economic policy toward either democratic or socialist countries. Adhering to international criteria, the ROC intends to employ its economic strength to expand foreign trade relations, to actively create new international space, and to enhance its international status. In terms of foreign investment, we have strengthened discipline and increased our combined energies. In terms of foreign trade, we have focused on expanding multilateral relations and balanced development. After many years of hard work, our foreign trade has become much more liberalized and internationalized.

As for trade relations with the Chinese mainland, however, the ROC's policy has had to take political factors into account so as to safeguard national security and meet the practical needs of overall economic development and private enterprises. This is because the Chinese communists have not eliminated their antagonism towards us. Under the structure of the *Guidelines for National Unification* and the prerequisite of "strengthening Taiwan before integrating with the mainland," we have progressively and indirectly promoted bi-coastal trade and economic exchanges based on the principles of pragmatism, steadiness and foresight. From now on, as we have gradually opened to the Chinese mainland, we will institutionalize the various kinds of trade and economic exchanges. In addition to strengthening our guidance for Taiwanese businessmen who are bound for the Chinese mainland, we will also provide them with a clear direction and a working model for them to follow, so that bi-coastal trade exchange can develop in the direction of benign interaction.

What are the Taipei government's economic priorities?

The domestic production environment, economic and trade system, and the international competitive advantage of the ROC all have changed rapidly in recent years. Developments such as the formation of international economic regions, restrictions inherent in the new international mechanisms, and the influence generated from the trade and economic interactions between the two sides of the Taiwan Straits have time and again challenged the ROC's economic development. In response, the ROC has to adjust its economic policies. At present, the ROC's economic priorities are as follows:

Domestically, the ROC will accelerate the upgrading of local industries and adjust its trade and economic policies. The ROC government will carry out the *Statutes for Industrial Upgrading*, use tax incentives to encourage the private sector to engage in R&D, introduce high-tech know-how from foreign countries, and establish an environment favorable to industrial upgrading. At the same time, the ROC will revise and formulate laws and regulations to meet the requirements of GATT and international environmental protection organizations. The ROC government will also assist local industries to adjust their structures so that the impact of these changes can be lessened.

Internationally, the ROC will set up an Asia-Pacific regional operations center and participate in international trade and economic organizations. The ROC government will accelerate the planning and construction of tangible and intangible assets such as telecommunications services, transportation links, financial systems, land taxes, and legal regulations, in order to encourage multinational companies to set up offices in Taiwan and introduce state-of-the-art technologies and management systems.

The ROC government will also use available resources and current conditions to announce to the international community its determination to participate in international organizations and to fulfill its responsibilities to the international community. We are preparing to enter GATT, and we will continue to participate in the unofficial seminars sponsored by the OECD. We would like to establish good relations with the World Bank and other international trade and economic organizations so we can participate in these organizations when the time is right.

In our relations with the other side of the Taiwan Straits, we will place equal stress on guidance and management. We will seek to legally institutionalize the trade and economic exchanges between the two sides of the Taiwan Straits.

In accordance with the principles of pragmatism, surefootedness, and foresight, the ROC government will promote benign interaction between the two sides of the Taiwan Straits and legally institutionalize the trade and economic exchanges between the two sides so as to spur reform on the Chinese mainland and thereby progress towards the goal of national unification.

On December 19, general elections were held and the ruling party, the Kuomintang, retained power. How

do you evaluate the election results — were they better or worse than the ruling party expected?

Overall, the 1992 event was a "maintaining election." The ruling party captured most of the votes and retained its majority position in the Legislative Yuan. Our analysis of voters' attitudes indicates that the basic picture of support for both the Kuomintang and the Democratic Progressive Party showed no noticeable change. Dedicated Kuomintang supporters still voted for KMT candidates in this election; however, the Democratic Progressive Party made a better grade in winning undecided voters than before.

Comparatively, the Republic of China has moved faster towards democracy over the last decade than other countries. Yet, in comparison with political parties in other countries that are aggressively promoting democracy, the Kuomintang has been the only ruling party able to consistently win a majority of the votes. This is the electorate's recognition of the achievements of the KMT over the years. The KMT is proud of this. The Kuomintang, like any other political party, local or foreign, hopes to gain as much support from the populace and as many votes as possible. The outcome of the 1992 elections did not all go as we would have wished. We will have to work harder than before. The steady development of the Democratic Progressive Party within the democratic system has a positive effect on spurring innovation and progress within the Kuomintang. It is a healthy development for democracy in the Republic of China.

What are the practical implications of your appointment as premier? Will there be any change of emphasis in government policy?

My appointment as premier marks a break from the past in several ways:

First, during the nomination process, the president, who is empowered to nominate the candidate for this office, sought the views of the legislators from both the ruling and the opposition parties. I was appointed after confirmation by the new parliament and will be subject to its supervision. This represents a change in the relations between the executive branch and the legislative branch, and truly realizes the spirit of political democratization. The party to which I belong conducted a series of discussions and negotiations. This indicates that the Kuomintang is responding to social change outside the party and is beginning to construct a model for intra-party democratic operations.

Second, before I assumed office as premier, I had served as a minister in the central government and as governor of the Taiwan Provincial Government. This shows that the candidate for premiership must fully understand the needs of the grassroots and take care of their interests, making a change of relations between the central government and the local government.

Third, due to developments in the world situation and relations between the two sides of the Taiwan Straits, the nation must throw away its historical baggage and usher in a new era in a more active spirit of reform. The appointment of the premier from among the middle-age generation ushers in a new era in the Republic of China.

During my tenure as premier, my administration will focus on the following policies:

First, we will adopt an active foreign policy. The ROC considers the recognition of the Chinese communist regime by a foreign country that maintains diplomatic relations simultaneously with the ROC as an internal affair of that country. The ROC always gives its first consideration to its national interests. The ROC will adopt a more active and positive strategy to develop room for international maneuver through multilateral activities and activities held by international organizations, especially regarding the issue of rejoining the United Nations.

Second, we will work towards perfecting our mainland China policy. Communist China continues to stifle us in our international activities, violating the spirit of the three-phase *Guidelines for National Unification*. The ROC government will, therefore, adopt a prudent but progressive policy in its promotion of bi-coastal contacts.

Third, we will adopt a realistic economic policy. We have reviewed the Six-Year National Development Plan launched two years ago, in order to make more effective use of resources. In addition, our government has come up with an Economic Stimulus Package to reverse a slowdown in investment in hopes of guiding economic development with government strength.

Our fourth objective is to establish a just society. The government will set up a comprehensive medical insurance system and a farmers' annuity system, expand social welfare resources, as well as strengthen environmental protection and natural conservation.

A number of different policy options have been debated for future relations with Beijing, ranging from "one China" to "two Chinas," not to mention the opposition's call for an independent "Republic of Taiwan." What is your favored policy?

First of all, the government of the Republic of China has advocated "one China" all the way. Of this, there can be no doubt. The "one China" we advocate is the Republic of China, which has existed since its establishment in 1912. The Republic of China has sovereignty over all of China but governs only Taiwan, Penghu, Kinmen, and Matsu.

Secondly, in pursuit of the development of the Chinese people, prosperity and strength for the nation, and the welfare of the people, the ROC government drafted and passed the *Guidelines for National Unification*, which actively solicits consensus between the Chinese people living on either side of the Taiwan Straits. We truly hope that the political authorities in the Chinese mainland will seek truth from facts, pragmatically shed their prejudices, and contribute their wisdom and their strength to work with us in building a free and democratic China with equitable prosperity.

Do you think "dual recognition," i.e., establishing diplomatic relations with countries which already recognize Beijing, is a viable policy option?

The Republic of China is a sovereign country which fulfills its international responsibilities. The ROC, of course, enjoys all the rights and privileges due to a sovereign country, including the right to establish diplomatic relations with other countries. Likewise, the countries with which we have developed relations are also sovereign countries. They have the right to choose whom they wish to have relations with. We should respect this. This means that the ROC has no say and no way to say if countries that have already recognized Peking choose to continue this recognition when they want to establish or re-establish diplomatic relations with us. Nevertheless, I would like to especially emphasize one point: The key to whether or not "dual recognition" is feasible is not the ROC or any country which would like to establish relations with us. It lies in the Chinese communists' refusal to face the fact that China has been divided for nearly half a century, their subjective assertion that they are the only legal government of China, and their utter disapproval of any realization of "dual recognition." Take for example, the ROC's establishment of diplomatic relations with Grenada on July 20, 1989. The ROC set up an embassy in the capital of Grenada on July 31 of that year, and the Chinese communists severed relations with Grenada on August 7. The ROC then established or re-established diplomatic relations with Liberia and six other countries. The Chinese communists followed by announcing that they were severing diplomatic relations with each of these countries. This clearly shows the consistent way in which the Chinese communists have sought to intimidate the international community and to isolate the Republic of China.

In view of the rapidly changing world situation, the ROC government is vigorously promoting pragmatic diplomacy to create new opportunities. Already, this policy has earned concrete results. The ROC will study issues such as "dual recognition" in order to better develop its diplomatic work on all fronts.

Are any foreign affairs initiatives planned for the near future, and if so, what direction would you like Taipei's foreign relations to take?

The ROC will resolutely press forward to attain its principal goal in foreign policy, which is participation in the United Nations. In line with the United Nations' principle of universality of membership, the 20.8 million people residing in the area under the effective control of the ROC deserve proper representation, as well as respect for their basic human rights. The ROC's participation in the United Nations is not just the common aspiration of the people in the ROC. The international community has everything to gain from it. The ROC's extraordinary achievements in economics, trade, and political democratization, as well as its technological and financial assistance to developing countries amply prove that the ROC is both willing and able to assume an active and constructive role in the international community. The ROC has participated in all forms of international activities, to the benefit of the international community.

If the ROC is barred from the United Nations and excluded from international treaties, the ROC will be hindered from contributing to international relief and economic development projects. This would surely be a great loss for the United Nations and the international community. To promote the ROC's entry into the United Nations, the Executive Yuan in February 1993 formed a United Nations Participation Policy Committee and the Ministry of Foreign Affairs set up a United Nations Participation Task Force. Banking on its economic and trade strength, the ROC will demonstrate its willingness to reciprocate to the international community and make active contributions in order to expand our international relations, seek support in the international community, and build up rapport within the United Nations. With support from the whole country, the ROC aspires to attain the goal of participating in the United Nations in the near future.

What initiatives would you suggest to settle the various outstanding security issues in the China Sea, such as the dispute over the Spratly Islands?

In terms of history, geography, international law, or actual fact, the Spratly Islands are part of the ROC territories. The ROC's sovereignty over these islands does not allow any doubt. Nevertheless, to avoid conflict and to maintain peace and security in the region, President Lee has suggested that countries work together to develop the Spratly Islands and to replace controversy with cooperation. The ROC is willing to contribute financial and technological assistance.

Accompanied by Kaohsiung City Mayor Wu Den-yih (center), the premier (second from the right) inspects the city's major construction projects on October 23, 1993.

Democratic, Economic and Diplomatic Challenges for the ROC

Responses to Questions Posed by the
Cable News Network, United States
April 10, 1993

Taiwan has just had an election that has been described as a milestone in the country's democratic development. What are the social and economic factors that made this development possible, and to what extent do they now make Taiwan the world's first genuinely democratic Chinese society? Further, what are the implications of this development not only for Taiwan but for the Chinese mainland as well?

I believe that the following socioeconomic factors are primarily responsible for the steady democratization of the Republic of China on Taiwan: continued economic prosperity, a high quality of living, a large middle-class, universal education, social pluralism, and the freedoms of assembly and association. Such factors have nurtured the autonomous decision-making abilities of the people and raised their interest in political participation. By joining various civic groups and political parties, and by participating in elections for government officials at the central and local levels, the public has to some extent developed democratic behaviors and a culture of democracy. This, in turn, has facilitated the moderate and gradual democratization of the Republic of China on Taiwan. I firmly believe that these factors will continue leading the way to the gradual establishment of a mature democratic system in Taiwan. In other words, these factors will allow the Chinese people in Taiwan to enjoy a lifestyle and political system of the people, by the people, and for the people. This political evolution will, of course, be a very influential model of development for the Chinese mainland. When they find that people in the Republic of China on Taiwan can enjoy a prosperous life and a free democratic system, the people in the Chinese mainland will pressure the Chinese communist authorities by asking themselves "Why Taiwan and not us?" Furthermore, judging from the ROC's experience in political and economic development, we can predict that when the Chinese communist authorities promote economic development, major changes in the mainland's socioeconomic structure will go hand in hand with rapid economic growth and that political liberalization and democratization will be certain to follow.

One of the consequences of this democratic progress has been to fuel more debate about a separate identity for Taiwan, and possibly even eventual independence. What is your view of this issue, especially given the Chinese communists' continuing threat to use force if Taiwan moves towards independence?

Democratization does not necessarily entail Taiwan's taking the road to independence. In fact, the vast majority of people in Taiwan continue to strongly identify with the Republic of China and look forward to the eventual reunification of the country. Taiwan's democratization only highlights the people's desire that the ROC be a sovereign and independent nation in the international community. We firmly reject the Chinese communists' claims that they represent all of China and that Taiwan is a part of the "People's Republic of China." The Chinese communists have no grounds for and are incapable of representing the ROC internationally. All the people of Taiwan want is the respect due to a country. They do not want to deny the existence of the Republic of China or to reject the ideal of eventual unification of the nation. We also hope that the Western democracies can respect the will of the Taiwan people which has been revealed through the process of political democratization: that the stature of the nation is promoted and that the prestige of the nation is upheld.

Despite continuing political differences, contact, trade and other links between Taiwan and the mainland have increased dramatically. Some analysts even talk about the long-term emergence of an economic unit consisting of Taiwan, the mainland and Hong Kong. How do you view this prospect? How important to Taiwan is the economic relationship with the mainland and to what extent do you see this process as contributing to a broader liberalization in mainland China?

Actually, the proposal to establish an economic entity formed by Taiwan, Hong Kong and mainland China reflects the increasingly close economic relations among the three areas. It is also a response to the global trend of regional economic alignments.

No conclusion on the formation of such an economic entity has yet been reached. The Chinese communist authorities stress that such an economic entity would signify economic coordination among the different regions within one China, and they have tried to base their political advocacy of "one country, two systems" on such a formation. However, we in the Republic of China on Taiwan believe that the economic entity should take the form of international economic integration and that the participants should continue to enjoy their independent and sovereign status.

In economic terms, these three areas are not as compatible or inter-dependent in trading relations with each other as they are with other trading partners. The formation of a common economic entity out of these three areas is, therefore, not highly beneficial. Besides, major differences exist between the consumer demand, income levels, and industrial infrastructures of each of the three areas. The establishment of an economic entity will not easily yield large-scale trade benefits within the industry. In other words, a longer period of time is needed before the prerequisites for the formation of an economic entity are in place

Furthermore, the establishment of an economic entity is restricted by many non-economic factors, such as opposing positions on the political sovereignty of the two sides of the Taiwan Straits, and the difficulties in working with each other that result from the different systems. Such factors hinder the formation of an economic entity.

The development of economic and trade relations with mainland China is important to the Taiwan area for the following reasons:

First, Taiwan and the Chinese mainland enjoy different comparative benefits and have different natural resources. The development of economic and trade relations across the Taiwan Straits would be economically beneficial to both sides, contributing to their economic prosperity, and providing an important channel for maintaining the development of harmonious relations between the two sides. One can predict that the market provided by the Chinese mainland will play an increasingly prominent role in Taiwan's economic development.

Second, any move towards economic integration affects the security of Taiwan. Peking's economic and trade policy towards Taiwan is directed at achieving the goal of "one country, two systems." The Chinese communists may also be using economic and trade exchanges to carry forward their Taiwan strategy of "achieving political ends via economic means." When developing economic and trade relations with the Chinese mainland, the ROC government must consider both economic benefits and national security if it is to ensure the welfare of the Taiwan society.

We hope that through the expansion of economic and trade exchanges across the Taiwan Straits, we can offer Chinese mainland the course and experience of Taiwan's economic success for reference and help the Chinese mainland promote its economic reforms. We hope that Taiwan's economic might may be employed to spur the liberalization and market-orientation of the Chinese mainland's economy. We also wish to cooperate with countries around the world to push forward the peaceful evolution of the Chinese mainland in hopes of creating a democratic, free, and equitably prosperous China.

For several years, Taiwan has been diplomatically isolated. That now seems to be changing. To what do you attribute this change, and what is your strategy to

take advantage of it? In addition, what hopes do you have of closer ties with the United States under the new Clinton administration?

The economic might of the ROC on Taiwan has allowed it to gradually free itself from diplomatic isolation. Now that the Cold War is over and the Soviet Union has disintegrated, Western countries no longer have to give in to the Chinese communists, and many former socialistic countries have extended the hand of friendship to the ROC on Taiwan. Today, countries around the world are directing greater attention to the international economy. Taiwan's economic strength naturally cannot be overlooked.

In the face of many changes in the international community, the ROC on Taiwan will still maintain its economic growth and adjust industrial structure so as to promote trade and economic exchanges between itself and countries the world over on a fairer and more mutually beneficial basis. We hope to contribute to the international community by enhancing bilateral relations between the ROC and other countries and by participating in multilateral organizations. We also hope that countries will begin to see logic and inevitability of the ROC's return to the international community.

President Clinton understands the ROC very well and is a politician of ideals and aspirations. I hope that the ROC and the United States can upgrade their relationship on a fair and mutually beneficial basis. I further expect that sincere cooperation between the ROC and the U.S. will help the U.S. to overcome its current economic difficulties and also help the ROC to put an early end to its diplomatic isolation.

Taiwan is often described as having achieved an "economic miracle" over recent years. What are the chief challenges you now face in ensuring that "miracle" continues through the rest of the decade?

Taiwan's "economic miracle" is actually the result of the steady efforts of its diligent people and entrepreneurs, combined with the appropriate financial and economic policies promoted by the ROC government. The administrative priority of the new cabinet shall be the transformation of the ROC into a progressive and modernized country with an annual per capital GNP of over US$20,000 before the dawn of the 21st century. In order to reach this objective, the ROC government is going to step up its implementation of the projects under the Six-Year National Development Plan which are creative and developmental in nature. Such projects include the upgrading of telecommunications and transportation infrastructure, creating a favorable investment environment, promoting industrial upgrading, and strictly carrying out the goal of liberalization and internationalization.

Nevertheless, it is undeniable that the continuous appreciation of the New Taiwan dollar, incessant rises in the wages of laborers, and the increasing need for environmental protection have, in recent years, lowered the international competitiveness of labor-intensive industries which were once the motors behind Taiwan's exports and rapid economic growth. Faced with these challenges in Taiwan's economic environment, local industries are swiftly converting into capital- and technology-intensive industries, which will be the key to maintaining the international competitiveness of Taiwan products. Taiwan will be challenged to strengthen its research and development, to cultivate people of talent, heighten its administrative efficiency, reform the way it levies taxes, overhaul the financial system, and modify out-dated laws. Taiwan must overcome these challenges if it is to create another "economic miracle."

The premier (center in gray jacket) listens attentively to Taiwan Provincial Governor James Soong expound the latest development of the Shihmen Dam on September 13, 1993.

The Outlook for Chinese Unification

Responses to Written Questions Submitted by
Focus Weekly, Germany
July 1993

With the appointment to the U.N., Taiwan strives to end diplomatic isolation. Do you also strive to re-establish a diplomatic relationship with Germany?

The Republic of China on Taiwan has a population of more than 20 million. It possesses considerable economic strength, and stresses democracy and respect for human rights. The international community should directly confront the fact that the Republic of China has long been barred from the United Nations, an extremely unreasonable situation. Based on the U.N. principle of universality of membership, our government and people are entitled to participate in the United Nations, and to contribute to the international community.

The Republic of China is a sovereign state and has striven all the way to establish diplomatic ties with major countries of the world. Therefore, the Republic of China treasures its relations with Germany. A unified Germany will play an increasingly important role in the international community and will enjoy broader diplomatic space in the post-Cold War era. I eagerly hope that this epochal change in the international environment will be conducive to improving and developing relations between the ROC and Germany.

Did Taiwan change its opinion towards economic cooperation with Germany after Bonn stopped the submarine-deal?

The ROC government has attached great importance to trade with Germany. Germany is our largest European trading partner. Total trade between the ROC and Germany reached US$7.52 billion in 1992.

The political reform and economic power of the Republic of China have gradually attracted the international community's attention. Other European countries have already set the precedent for selling arms to the ROC. We hope that the German government will reconsider its position on the sale of submarines to the ROC government. The ROC government fully recognizes the importance and influence of Germany in the European Community. In the future, we hope to strengthen trade relations with Germany. We are confident that both the Republic of China and Germany will greatly benefit from this effort.

What do you expect from Germany regarding economic relations?

First, we look forward to your support for our entry into international organizations. The ROC's application to enter GATT has won positive support from your country and other advanced Western nations. I am very grateful for this, and I hope that you will continue to support our efforts to join other international economic organizations such as the OECD and the World Bank.

Next, we also hope that you will transfer technologies to the ROC. We are presently diversifying our import sources in order to reduce our reliance on Japan.

We hope that your country will export high-tech products through technological transfers to help us upgrade our industries and promote our bilateral trade relations.

Finally, we hope that you will encourage German businessmen to make Taiwan the center of their operations in the Asia-Pacific region. We have a high-quality work force, ample capital, well-developed sales channels, and a wealth of experience. We welcome German entrepreneurs to use these advantages to develop the Asia-Pacific market from a base of operations in Taiwan.

Do you recognize the possibility of German-Taiwanese investment on the mainland?

Our government limits our trade with the Chinese mainland and our investment there to the private sector and follows an "indirect" way as envisaged for the short-term phase of the *Guidelines for National Unification*. We will relax these restrictions in an orderly and gradual manner, and to a degree in keeping with the response from the Chinese mainland. We do not rule out the possibility of permitting private organizations such as the Straits Exchange Foundation to set up branches on the Chinese mainland.

The political instability of the Chinese communists, the absence of an institutionalized system, and inconsistencies in policy caused by personnel changes have deprived Taiwan businessmen of credible guarantees. The ROC government at the current stage does not encourage Taiwan investment in the mainland, thus joint German-Taiwanese investment in the Chinese mainland is still out of question. Nevertheless, should the mainland respond to our moves positively, we could

217

then be able to consider or assess the feasibility of investing in the Chinese mainland jointly with Germany or other countries.

Do talks between Peking and Taipei in Singapore represent a first step towards the recognition of two Chinas?

The ROC government authorized the Straits Exchange Foundation to engage in consultations with the Chinese mainland's Association for Relations Across the Taiwan Straits in order to resolve problems arising from bi-coastal private-sector exchanges. The intention was to institutionalize channels for consultation so that problems and disputes could be resolved step by step, and mutual understanding and trust between the people on Taiwan and the mainland could be strengthened, thereby creating a climate for national unification. The SEF and ARATS discussed practical and functional matters, without touching upon political issues, much less the question of "two Chinas."

Ever since the Republic of China was established in 1912, our government has staunchly adhered to the "one China" policy. We adamantly oppose "one China, one Taiwan," even though our country has been divided since 1949. We now have two political entities governing the Taiwan area and the mainland area respectively. This is an objective reality that no calls for unification can disregard.

In which areas do you expect the Peking authorities to make a favorable response?

By positive response, we expect Peking to adhere to the principles of reason, peace, parity, and reciprocity in handling bi-coastal relations. Specifically, in the realm of policy, the Chinese communists should respond to our sincerity in terminating the Period of National Mobilization for Suppression of the Communist Rebellion by renouncing the use of armed force against Taiwan and committing themselves to peaceful solution of all bi-coastal disputes. The Chinese communists should acknowledge the political reality of China's temporary division and recognize us as an equal political entity. In the international arena, we should respect, not discriminate against, each other. In terms of administrative affairs, they should not deliberately disrupt normal private-sector exchanges between Taiwan and the Chinese mainland with contrived issues. Instead, they should allow reciprocal information exchanges and liberalize the expression of opinion so as to establish a consensus on the democratic unification of China and lay a foundation for the future social system and lifestyle of the Chinese people.

A favorable response from the Chinese communists at the administrative level will have a direct impact on the development of Taiwan-mainland exchanges and mutual trust. In addition, a favorable policy response from Peking will directly boost the progress of bi-coastal relations as set forth in the *Guidelines for National Unification* and will advance the mid-term phase of official contacts and mutual trust and cooperation.

Dressed in the traditional
garb of a tribe indigenous
to Taiwan, the premier visits eastern Taiwan on April
19, 1993.

The Prospective Course of Cross-Straits Relations and Regional Development

An Interview Conducted by Peter Seidlitz,
Far East & China Correspondent, *Handelsblatt*, Germany
October 1993

The view about the perspective of mainland China is very contradictory. Some people are saying the country is going to sink into economic chaos and even civil war again. Others see it already as the third largest economy in the world and a new superpower. What is your view?

The future of mainland China hinges on whether or not it can smoothly and peacefully reform its economic and political systems. To quickly develop the economy, the Chinese communists have in recent years adopted a policy of skewed development that emphasizes industry over agriculture and the coastal areas over the inland, thus creating a burgeoning disparity between urban and rural development. In farms and villages, farmers are taking to violence to vent their dissatisfaction with the government's onerous levies and various taxes, while in the cities law and order is deteriorating. In addition, excessive growth of the monetary supply and an overheated economy due to a rise in the Chinese communist fiscal deficit have led to price hikes and have spurred inflation.

Attracting greater amounts of foreign investment is currently the major economic policy of the Chinese communists. However, their negligence of infrastructural

223

facilities, such as roads, ports, electricity and energy, as well as the proper coordination of the raw materials supply have caused a gradual deterioration in the investment environment. Furthermore, Chinese communist rule on the mainland lacks a legal foundation; it is mostly oligarchical. Despite more than ten years of reform and liberalization, investment laws and regulations there are still unsound. Thus, without the sufficient legal guarantees, foreign investors are adopting a wait-and-see attitude. Economic development and political reform are two sides of the same coin. The experience of developing nations demonstrates that if political and economic reform do not go hand in hand, they will inevitably fail. The Chinese communists are currently mired in this chaotic state. Only if the Chinese communists implement democracy and the rule of law will the prospects for their economic development be bright.

Do you believe that the Chinese communists can manage political reforms and will eventually allow democratization?

The Chinese communists have always feared that peaceful evolution and liberalization of thinking would pose a threat to their mainland communist regime. With growing economic development, improvements in the standard of living for their people, and gradual formation of a professional and middle class in their society, the Chinese communists are bound to face the pressure of demands for political liberalization upon the heels of economic development like that experienced in other developing nations. However, democratic liberalization in politics is tantamount to terminating the system of

dictatorship by the Chinese Communist Party, hence the

stubborn resistance by the Chinese communists to the trend of liberalization and democracy. Therefore, during the 1989 Pro-Democracy Movement, what were originally nothing more than simple appeals by students and the public against bribery and corruption ultimately resulted in the bloody Tienanmen Incident, because the Chinese communists feared that the movement was a challenge to their authority.

The Chinese communist authorities have recently invented a new term, "market economy with socialist characteristics," in the hope that after reform and liberalization, the economy would still be under the control of the Chinese Communist Party's authority, and the two mutually contradictory systems would meld into one. However, this has formed obstacles to the functioning of this economic system. The difficulties inherent in such a combined system are numerous and so obvious that they need not be discussed further.

The ROC government hopes that the Chinese communist authorities, after doing all they can to achieve economic reform and liberalization, will continue with democratic reform and liberalizations of their politics. We further hope that such political reforms can start with the self-enlightenment of the Chinese communist leaders themselves. We are very willing to provide our developmental experience to help mainland China start down the road toward democracy, freedom and equitable prosperity.

Have you learned here in Taipei any lessons from the German unification? Unification has been ruinous and expensive for Germany, and if Korea or China unite,

it will be even more expensive. Can you afford it or would you not be better off alone?

The division of Germany was originally the result of international factors and is not the same as the situation involving the two sides of the Taiwan Straits. Although these two cases cannot be dealt with in an exactly comparable fashion, this experience and process of a divided nation being able to achieve reunification through peaceful means has profound instructive significance for the future reunification of China. German reunification triggered some local social unrest, and since then, the country has encountered many economic problems. This has shown that forcing reunification on two different societies which have a wide gap in economic standards, political systems, and social development only creates new problems and unrest. The two sides must therefore wait until they have narrowed the gap in these various areas before proceeding with reunification. Germany's experience with reunification has left us more convinced than before that we have rightly adopted the policy of achieving reunification in the gradual phases defined in the *Guidelines for National Unification*. The task of national reunification is a long and arduous political process which cannot be achieved overnight or in a short period of time. Many glaring differences in ideology, social systems, and lifestyle have emerged over the more than forty years of division between the two sides of the Taiwan Straits. This situation is compounded by the Chinese communists' refusal to relinquish their plan to take Taiwan by force. Hence, the time is still not ripe for the reunification of China.

The reunification of China is the common wish of the Chinese people at home and abroad. The two sides of the Taiwan Straits should gradually proceed through the various phases of reunification with reason, peace, equality, and mutual exchange, and should attain reunification by first undergoing an appropriate period of frank and sincere exchanges, cooperation, and dialogue. In the current short-term phase, the ROC will promote understanding through exchanges, and dissolve enmity through reciprocity, in the hope that the Chinese mainland will actively promote economic reform, liberalize the expression of public opinion, and implement democracy and the rule of law. When in the future progress in democratization and economic liberalization on the Chinese mainland finally narrows the gap between the two sides of the Taiwan Straits, then over time the conditions and environment will become ripe for the reunification of China. This gradual method of reunification can minimize the cost thereof.

Since the Chinese communists have neither abandoned the "four cardinal principles" nor renounced the use of force against Taiwan, but instead stick to their "one country, two systems" policy, and are always scheming to reduce the ROC to a local government and do away with its room for activities in the international community, it is therefore impossible for the ROC to change its policy of "no contact, no negotiation, and no compromise" between the ROC and the Chinese communist authorities. The results of several public opinion surveys conducted in the Taiwan area show that the vast majority of the public approves of keeping the situation between the two sides of the Taiwan Straits as it is for the moment until the conditions are favorable and the time is ripe for the two sides to discuss the issue of reunification.

Why can't people of the same race, language and culture live in different countries? Look at Austria and Germany.

East and West Germany reunited after more than four decades of division, not just because the people are of one race, but principally because reunification was the common wish of the German people on both sides. That China today is divided for the moment with separate political systems is an objective reality. Many public opinion surveys conducted in the Taiwan area have shown that the majority of people approve of reunification at an opportune time in the future. It is reported that similar surveys conducted on the Chinese mainland also indicate that the vast majority of people think that China should be united. I believe that the desire for reunification by Chinese people on both sides of the Straits is crucial to our task of promoting the reunification of China.

The ROC advocates that national reunification should most importantly, by its very process, be to the mutual benefit of the Chinese people on both sides of the Taiwan Straits. For the sake of the 1.2 billion people on the Chinese mainland, the ROC advocates that conditions should be improved so that these people can also enjoy the same democratic, free, and equitably prosperous lifestyle as do the people in the Taiwan area. Likewise, for the sake of the people in the Taiwan area, the ROC asserts that determination of the timing and method of reunification must first honor the rights and interests of the people in the Taiwan area and assure their safety and welfare. As President Lee once stressed, "Economically, the mainland is Taiwan's hinterland." Therefore, the ROC is working to advance cross-Straits relations with an eye to mutual benefit and reciprocity.

How do you think history should and will judge old communist leaders like Deng Xiaoping? He seems to come around in old age and is making a turnaround.

Although the economic reforms pushed by Deng Xiaoping in his latter years have their value and have achieved some results, the Tienanmen Massacre he spearheaded in 1989 remains an indelible stain in history. During their "14th Party Congress" last year, the Chinese communists still maintained their allegiance to Marxism-Leninism-Maoism and the leadership of the CCP, only stressing a partial administrative reworking while rejecting political reform. We feel that it would be conducive to the future reunification of the two sides if Deng Xiaoping in his remaining years could be more forward-looking and decisive, and would courageously get on with political reform, implement democracy, pragmatically give up the "one country, two systems" notion, accept the fact that there are two equal political entities across the Taiwan Straits, and respond positively with good will, mutual trust and equality. Otherwise, all that Deng Xiaoping in his late years has striven to achieve will amount to nothing more than consolidating the Chinese communist regime by means of economic reforms, for he has failed to take the entire Chinese people into consideration, and even more has proven lacking in the requisite vision and know-how for Chinese reunification.

In the old day there was the policy of "three nos." This policy seems to be eroded by your business community. Are you going to open up totally or are there still some "nos"?

Our government's policy of "three nos" means no government-to-government or official-to-official contact, negotiation or compromise. Cross-Straits economic, cultural or athletic activities, however, belong to the domain of private-sector exchange, and are distinct from the official "three nos" policy. At present, there are no prohibitions on such private-sector exchanges; we hope that, through those non-governmental activities, cross-Straits information exchange will intensify and hostility will be reduced, thereby helping the two sides move toward a stage of mutual trust and cooperation, and to gradually establish an environment conducive to the ultimate goal of national reunification. However, the Chinese communists have not publicly renounced the use of force against Taiwan, and have always held an unrealistic attitude of regarding us as a local government, constantly putting the squeeze on our room for maneuver in international activities. So, were our government to abandon its "three nos" policy on its own initiative at this juncture, it would in fact be very unrealistic.

What were the sticking points in the Chinese-Chinese talks in Singapore? What are the next steps?

During the talks, the delegates for the two sides were unable to reach a common understanding on economic exchanges or on guarantees of the rights and interests of Taiwan businessmen. Nonetheless, they agreed to name the document on which they did reach a consensus the

Koo-Wang Talks Joint Accord. Regretfully, the Chinese communist side ignored the mutual understanding in the preparatory meetings by raising the issues of "direct transport, mail and trade" and labor cooperation for inclusion in the meeting agenda. This act unnecessarily increased the sense of antipathy and mistrust toward their side on the part of the whole citizenry in the Taiwan area, causing a setback in the talks.

Nonetheless, the Koo-Wang Talks have laid the foundation for regular cross-Straits private-sector exchange. We hope that through negotiation we can reach a mutual understanding and arrive at methods to resolve problems resulting from cross-Straits exchange. In the future, the two sides will further devote their efforts to realizing the content of the agreement, and, it is hoped, cross-Straits relations can — on this basis — lead to a working out of peaceful, reasonable, equal and reciprocal methods to gradually increase the kind and scope of cross-Straits exchanges.

Taiwan airlines are ready for the China-China traffic. Why are you hesitating to give the OK for direct flights?

The opening up of direct flights or shipping link between the two sides of the Taiwan Straits requires the signing of an air and sea transportation agreement between the governments on each side of the Straits. Only in this way can flight and shipping safety be assured and the requisite order for air and sea transportation be established.

At the current stage when the Chinese communists have not relinquished the use of military force against

Taiwan, do not recognize the ROC on Taiwan as an equal political entity, and pressure us about every activity in the international community whenever they can, the two sides have no way on an equal basis to hold talks about an air and sea transportation agreement fairly and reasonably. Thus, issues regarding air and navigational rights, air and shipping lines, disputes settlement, tax, customs checking, and certification for ship registry cannot be resolved satisfactorily, nor is there any way for our concerns for the safety of ROC airplanes and ships to be addressed.

The ROC has made preparations for direct air and sea links between the two sides of the Straits and has included such an issue in the medium-term phase of the *Guidelines for National Unification*. Direct air and sea links will be opened up after the aforementioned concerns are resolved and when guarantees are implemented. While any of the obstacles mentioned above remain unresolved, then I am afraid that direct transportation across the Taiwan Straits will not be feasible.

Are you satisfied with investment guarantees or do you fear that the expansion of Taiwan business community into the mainland is dangerous insofar as you are getting depended on the mainland?

The increasing intensity of trade relations between the two sides of the Taiwan Straits has resulted in an annual increase of indirect trade volume between the two sides and an expansion of Taiwan business investment in the mainland area, both in terms of the number of companies from Taiwan investing and the amount invested. As a result, the economies of the two sides are becoming increasingly interdependent.

Although economic reforms are already underway in the Chinese mainland, regulations there on foreign investment are not comprehensive enough, administrative efficiency is very low, corruption is rampant, and most public facilities cannot meet the demand of foreign investors, making it impossible for the rights and interests of investors from Taiwan to be duly protected. In July 1988, the Chinese communists came out with *Regulations on the Encouragement of Investment by Fellow Countrymen from Taiwan*. However, the *Regulations* have a very low legal status and are rife with many unclear and unreasonable sections. For this reason, during the Koo-Wang Talks held in Singapore, the ROC representatives not only asked the Chinese communist authorities to improve their legal and administrative systems and implement their enforcement, the ROC delegation also strove for the signing of a cross-Straits investment protection agreement in order to more reasonably and completely protect the investment rights and interests of Taiwan businessmen in mainland China. However, the Chinese communists refused to sign such an agreement.

Investment by Taiwan businesses in mainland China is indeed increasing rapidly. While this can help the Chinese mainland carry out its economic reforms and can allow our mainland compatriots to enjoy a modern lifestyle at an early date, it is hard not to worry about the accumulation of risk when such investment gets hasty and overheated. Especially as long as the Chinese communist regime remains stuck in a hostile mentality toward the ROC, and most recently has instituted a series of financial tightening measures due to the steep depreciation of the *renminbi* and the overheating of the

Chinese mainland economy that have added to the economically chaotic situation there, the risk for investments by Taiwan businesses in the Chinese mainland is accordingly far greater than in any other area. Therefore, we must proceed cautiously.

Free trade is in danger as more and more countries impose barriers against foreign goods. Are you worried about that development and does this lead to a China/ Asia/Japan block to counter NAFTA and the EEC?

The international situation has changed greatly since the end of the Cold War, and regional economic organizations have gradually arisen, replacing military antagonism with economic interests as the core of a reconstituted new world order. The heart of the world economy is also gradually shifting from the European Community and North America to the Asia-Pacific region. That the economy of the Asia-Pacific region has attracted increasing world attention in recent years can mainly be attributed to the powerful economic potential and rapid economic growth of this region. Nonetheless, the integration of the European Community and the establishment of NAFTA have also stepped up the pressure from the resultant competition.

Because of differences in political, financial, legal, defense, racial, religious, and cultural backgrounds throughout the Asia-Pacific region, there are variations in the extent of economic growth. Although the economy of the Chinese mainland is growing rapidly, there are indications of overheating, and financial problems have occurred. The Japanese economy has not recovered across the board yet, nor is the political situation there fully stable. Thus, at a juncture when the Chinese mainland and Japan are both facing difficulty after difficulty with their domestic economies, it is best in the near term to seek cooperation through bilateral or multilateral talks (such as the APEC forum). At present, it is still too early to talk about the formation of an economic bloc in the Asia-Pacific region to take on the European Community.

As for the North American Free Trade Area, since the U.S. plays an extremely important role in the APEC conference, and both North America and the European Community are presently the main export markets for products made by Asia-Pacific countries, the Asia-Pacific region and NAFTA should go all out to cooperate and provide mutual assistance, and to avoid developing antagonism. Nonetheless, market competition is naturally unavoidable.

What political role should Japan play in the region and could you foresee a communist Chinese/Japanese alliance in view of the very grave dispute the American government has with both mainland China and Japan?

First, the Cold War era has drawn to a close and countries around the world are vigorously reconstituting a new order. American and Russian power in Asia is gradually diminishing while Japan is gradually building up its influence in Asia, and even the world, as an economic superpower. Japan will play an important role, whether in terms of economics, politics, or the safeguarding of regional security. This is evidenced by its recent participation in U.N. peace-keeping operations.

However, as Japan is moving from being an economic superpower to becoming a political superpower, and especially because it is eager to become a permanent member of the U.N. Security Council, other Asian countries are wary of its moves because of their tragic historical experience of Japanese military invasion. Japan should, thus, dedicate itself to dispelling these concerns, take the feelings of other Asian nations into consideration, and with true sincerity and positive actions, make a concrete contribution to Asian regional peace and security. Only then will it be able to establish relations of mutual trust, mutual assistance, and mutual benefit with other Asian countries.

Secondly, although the United States, the Chinese mainland, and Japan continue to harbor many differences on such issues as regional politics, bilateral trade, and arms sales, the U.S. is actively seeking a balance of power throughout the Asia-Pacific region in order to maintain regional stability in Asia during the post-Cold War era. As Japan and the Chinese mainland are politically and economically interdependent, it is natural that Japan hopes to gain Peking's support in its efforts to become a permanent member of the U.N. Security Council, while the Chinese communists must rely on Japan to provide capital and technical assistance in their economic development. Therefore, both Japan and the Chinese mainland place emphasis on integrated interests and benefits and are inclined towards developing and maintaining stable relations.

In reality, however, their bilateral relations are potentially threatened by such controversial issues as their dispute over the sovereignty of the Tiaoyütai Islands and also by such practical problems as the Chinese communist military expansion. Trade disputes over opening markets remain between the U.S. and Japan, while there are controversies between the U.S. and mainland China over such issues as arms proliferation and human rights. All these are sure to become thorny issues for the three parties in their future relationships. But out of considerations for maintaining regional peace and stability and building a new world order, even though there may be frictions, these will not cause their multilateral relations to deteriorate. Accordingly, the factors for a Japanese/ Chinese communist alliance do not exist at the moment.

Many countries are disarming, not so Taiwan and mainland China. Is there still a real military threat and how could a confrontation develop?

The Chinese communists have increased their national defense spending year after year recently to allow themselves the ability to modernize their military. Twenty-four group armies now form the core of their ground forces. The Chinese communist navy has switched from an inshore configuration to an offshore offensive and defensive fighting navy. In addition to purchasing Soviet Su-27 jet fighters with an 800-mile offshore range, the Chinese communist air force is presently researching and manufacturing in-flight refueling planes and early-warning aircraft equipment. Thus there are predictions that by the year 2000, the Chinese mainland will have become a new hegemonic power in the Asian region. This has caused concern and fear among Asia-Pacific countries and has gradually raised the military threat to other countries in the region, surely having a negative effect upon the political and economic development of the region. In contrast, the objective of modernizing the ROC military is to establish an effective force for defense and deterrence. Only if we have a solid defense can we protect and maintain the independence and security of the nation. Only with adequate deterrent strength can we minimize the possibility of conflict. As the U.S. military is gradually withdrawing from the Asia-Pacific region, and the level of instability in the area is increasing, it has become even more important for the ROC to modernize its armed forces.

As China has suffered from colonialism for over a century, I would like to ask you if you are not glad to see the British finally leave Hong Kong?

Hong Kong is a part of Chinese territory. Hong Kong Island and the Kowloon Peninsula were ceded to England in 1842 and 1860 respectively because of unequal treaties, while the New Territories were leased to the British for 99 years beginning in 1898. Since the founding of the ROC in 1912, we have had the abrogation of the unequal treaties and the recovery of Chinese territory as our goal. But because Great Britain has diplomatic relations with the Chinese communists, it has been negotiating with Peking on the Hong Kong issue. The ROC government does not recognize any agreement signed between the Chinese communists and Great Britain, but is positively disposed toward Hong Kong's release from colonial rule. We hope that Hong Kong will be able to pursue political democracy while preserving its prosperity, stability, and freedom. Only then will the situation be a blessing for our Chinese compatriots in Hong Kong and Macau.